Son
of the
Promise

Shirley Ballantine

Son Of The Promise
by Shirley Ballantine

Printed in the United States of America.

ISBN 9781498483438

Scripture quotations taken from the New International Version (NIV). Copyright © 1982 by International Bible Society. Used by permission. All rights reserved.

Scripture quotations taken from the New King James Version (NKJV). Copyright © 1982 by Thomas Nelson, Inc. Used by permission. All rights reserved.

www.xulonpress.com

Dedication

This book is dedicated to the memory of my lovely gentle dad, William Morrison, who passed on his love of the Scriptures to me, his eldest daughter.

Chapter 1

———— ❋ ————

*I*t all began in a garden, an exquisitely beautiful garden. The Creator of the garden was a perfectionist. That was his nature. The touch of his master hand was faultless. His garden was a place of incomparable beauty, joy and delight.

Since he was also a kind and generous Creator he wanted to share his garden with others, so he invited a man and a woman to be gardeners in his beautiful creation so that they could look after it and enjoy it.

Everything the pair could possibly need or want was there. Delicious fruit, berries and herbs flourished in abundance. Magnificent trees of every variety grew there, along with delightful flowers of every colour and hue. It was a haven for brightly-coloured birds who sang joyously in the branches. The air was pure and clean, and warm and pleasant in the sunshine. There was even a river running through the garden, reflecting the bluest of skies in the clear water.

From the gentle serenity of sunrise to the exuberant splendour of sunset, the garden catered to every mood. All around was colour and vibrancy, yet peace and tranquility.

The couple loved their life in the splendid garden. The Creator did not dictate to them what they should do. He gave them freedom of choice. They could wander at will through the trees, swim in the river, pick the flowers, gather the fruit, and enjoy everything the Creator had made.

In addition to all the wonderful things in the garden which they could enjoy, the man and the woman were endowed with intelligence, talents and skills.

There was only one thing the Creator withheld from them because he knew it would harm them, so he asked them not to seek the one piece of knowledge he had not given them.

He specifically told them, "You must not . . ." and warned them that if they did they would certainly die.

They did not know what it meant to die. They were alive and full of the joy of life. It was inconceivable that they would want anything to change.

Life continued thus for a time in the garden. Daily the man and the woman enjoyed to the full everything the Creator had given them.

In the evening when the day was done they met with him, and they talked together as friends and enjoyed each other's company. Life was joyously happy, completely perfect and wonderfully good.

Then one day something that was not good happened in the garden. A stranger entered. In reality he was an extremely wicked being, but he disguised himself so that the woman gardener, to whom he addressed himself, had no idea that he was full of evil intent. She and her husband had only ever experienced truth, goodness and love from their friend the Creator. They were not familiar with anything other than these qualities.

"Did God really say 'You must not'?" he insinuated cleverly.

He had made her think, so she paused before replying.

"God did say, 'You must not . . or you will die'," she told him.

"You will not die," the stranger lied.

He said it so smoothly and confidently that he caught her attention.

"God knows . . . you will be like God, knowing good and evil," he said, lowering his voice to sound reassuring.

It was tempting. To know everything, like God! Would that not be amazing! The stranger had put an intriguing idea into her head, and not knowing that he was completely duping her she fell for his lies, and shared the idea with her husband. The knowledge the stranger suggested seemed desirable since it would make them like God. So, in their ambition and foolishness, they did the very thing the Creator had asked them not to do.

But they had made a great mistake. They should have trusted the Creator.

Their action destroyed everything. They had broken faith with their friend the Creator, and as a result they had ruined their relationship with him. He had given them everything they needed and more, but they failed to trust him, heeding instead the lying stranger who only wanted to destroy them. In listening to him they had also desecrated the Creator's perfect creation, and nothing was ever the same again.

So the ugliness of sin came into the world, death became a reality, and life was no longer perfect.

What would God do now?

Well, God had a plan.

Chapter 2

———— ✳ ————

*G*od knew exactly who the stranger was who had entered the garden and corrupted the man and the woman. He was his enemy Satan, who had set himself up against God, and whose aim was to destroy everything that God had created, especially the humans.

The man and the woman were not guiltless, but God knew Satan was behind it.

It was not in God's nature to allow His enemy to gain the upper hand, and He would not leave His world without hope, so He began to put His plan into action.

"Because you have done this," He told Satan, "cursed are you . . . I will put enmity between you and the woman, and between your offspring and hers; he will crush your head, and you will strike his heel."

Listening, the man and the woman took heart from this pronouncement. God had cursed Satan, but in doing so He had given them hope.

Who was "he" who would crush the head of Satan?

Well, the world would have to wait a long time for his appearance, but when God promises something He brings it to pass. The day would come when "he" would appear and crush Satan.

Meanwhile, God in His mercy showed kindness to the man and the woman. Although they had to bear the consequences of their wrongdoing, God would not leave them desolate.

First of all He clothed them. This was a deeply significant act, because with it He would establish a pattern of atonement for sin which would last until "he" of the promise would come.

In order to cover them, God made garments of skin for the man and woman. He did this by killing some of the animals He had created. Their blood was shed so that covering could be provided for the humans, not merely covering for their bodies, but covering for their sin. From henceforth animals would have to be sacrificed to atone for the sins of human beings.

With this animal sacrifice came God's forgiveness. It was God's way, and gave a foretaste of the far distant future when God would fully demonstrate how His forgiveness would be achieved.

It was not God's wish to kill the creatures He had made, but neither was it His wish that death of any kind would enter His perfect creation. That was the doing of the man and the woman who had listened to the lies of a stranger instead of trusting the Friend whom they knew.

Finally, God decreed that the woman would give birth to children which encouraged both her and her husband and gave them hope for the future. In the light of that promise the man, Adam named his wife Eve, because she would become the mother of all living.

"The offspring of the woman" would crush the head of the serpent, Satan. By this, Adam and Eve knew that God fully intended to carry out His threat against Satan. It would be done through the offspring of the "woman". It was she who had fallen first, so it would be through her offspring that redemption would finally come.

After God had cursed Satan and spelled out the consequences of their sin to Adam and Eve, He expelled them from the garden, and they went out into a very different world, a fallen world. There they would face hardship and toil, pain and distress as they struggled in a broken world which was the result of their sin.

But they had hope, and they knew God still cared for them.

God's pronouncement to the evil one became known as the Protoevangelium, the first promise of a Saviour. As the first it is deeply significant since it demonstrates right from the beginning that God did have a plan to bring redemption to a fallen world.

The amazing truth is that He would use human beings to bring His plan to fulfillment, humans who had failed to trust Him and who had desecrated His beautiful creation. All who followed Adam and Eve inherited their sinful nature, but with God there is forgiveness, and He loves it when we come to Him and ask for His forgiveness.

It all began in a garden. Where would it end?

Chapter 3

The Protoevangelium was the first promise God gave that He would send a Saviour to crush Satan and rescue a fallen world. There would be many others.

"I will make you into a great nation and I will bless you; I will make your name great, and you will be a blessing. . . . . **And all peoples on earth will be blessed through you.**"

The man to whom these words were spoken was a descendant of Adam and Eve, who lived hundreds of years after they had turned to dust.

Abraham with his wife Sarah had left their own country at God's behest, and had come to a land God promised to give them.

"To your offspring I will give this land," God told them.

The trouble was that at seventy-five and sixty-five years old respectively, they did not have any children. They deeply longed for a child, especially Sarah, but as the years went by it seemed more and more unlikely. Yet, God had promised.

It would be another twenty-five years before Sarah would have the joy of holding the longed-for and promised baby in her arms.

Abraham was ninety-nine years old when God spoke amazing words to him. Among many promises God had given him, this time He spoke to him regarding his wife Sarah.

"I will bless her and will surely give you a son by her. I will bless her so that she will be the mother of nations; kings of people will come from her."

God even told Abraham what he was to call his son.

When both Abraham and Sarah laughed to themselves at the thought of having a child at their age, God said, "Is anything too hard for the Lord?"

Sarah was ninety years old when the miracle happened! She was so delighted that she laughed out of sheer joy.

"God has brought me laughter," she declared, "and everyone who hears about this will laugh with me."

God had begun to unfold His plan. He was beginning a family tree that would eventually lead to "he" of the first promise in the garden.

So Isaac was born. His name, which God had chosen for him before his birth, meant "laughter". God really has a sense of humour!

But it was more than just a little piece of humour. There was significance in it. A woman, the matriarch of this special family, had given birth to a son who was the forerunner of the one to come, the "he" of the promise.

The laughter was appropriate for it meant rejoicing; not just the happiness of a woman being blessed with a much-longed-for child, but a woman blessed with an offspring who was part of the plan God had put in place to rescue His fallen world.

17

Abraham and Sarah were richly blessed through the birth of their son Isaac, but they were not the only ones. The whole world would be blessed through the birth of this child.

"I will establish my covenant with him as an everlasting covenant for his descendants after him," declared God.

This covenant would endure until "he" of the promise would come.

Once more God told Abraham, "Through your offspring all nations on earth will be blessed."

Chapter 4

$\mathcal{B}$ecause of the importance of the promise that God had given him, Abraham was determined that Isaac would marry within his family circle which was part of the believing community who worshipped the Lord God, so some time after Sarah's death, when Isaac was about forty, Abraham called his chief servant to him.

"Go to my country and my own relatives and get a wife for my son Isaac," Abraham instructed his servant.

The beautiful young woman whom the chief servant brought back for Isaac was called Rebekah, and Isaac married her and loved her and found her to be a great comfort to him after the death of his mother.

God spoke to Isaac too as He had done to Abraham.

"I will make your descendants as numerous as the stars in the sky, and will give them all these lands, and **through your offspring all nations on earth will be blessed**."

Isaac and Rebekah eventually had twin sons, Jacob and Esau.

God had spoken to Rebekah before their birth and had told her, "the older will serve the younger."

Jacob was born just after Esau, making him the younger, but since God had chosen him before his birth, subsequently when the boys were grown up he was the one who received the traditional blessing which was passed from father to son.

This was not without complications however. Esau soon showed his displeasure at being cheated out of his birthright, and consequently Jacob had to flee for his life.

Isaac instructed him, "Go to the house of your mother's father Bethuel. Take a wife for yourself there. . . May God Almighty bless you and make you fruitful and increase your numbers until you become a community of peoples."

So Jacob went on a journey to his mother's people, and when he stopped for the night and lay down to sleep under the open sky, he had a dream.

Who has not heard of Jacob's ladder? In his dream he saw a stairway reaching from earth to heaven with angels ascending and descending upon it. At the top of the ladder stood the Lord, and the words He spoke to Jacob were similar to the same extraordinary blessing He had previously given to Jacob's father and grandfather before him.

"I am the Lord, the God of your father Abraham and the God of Isaac. I will give you and your descendants the land in which you are lying. Your descendants will be like the dust of the earth . . . **All peoples on earth will be blessed through you and your offspring.**"

Jacob was awed when he awoke. He spoke reverently.

"Surely the Lord is in this place and I was not aware of it."

Sometimes God touches the hearts of those who are barely aware of Him. He is not far from any one of us, and often He speaks when we least expect it.

This was Jacob's awakening and his response was, "How awesome is this place!"

Before he left the sacred spot he set up a stone there and called the place Bethel, house of God, and promised that if God would bless him and keep him safe He would be his God.

God had now reinforced His promise to Abraham, Isaac and Jacob that all peoples would be blessed through them. These men were the patriarchs of the promise, their wives were the matriarchs of the promise, and this promise would follow each succeeding generation until "he" whom God had promised would finally come.

After Jacob's deep spiritual experience when he received God's promised blessing, not just for himself but for "all peoples", he continued his journey to his mother's people. There he fell in love with his beautiful cousin Rachel, but was duped into marrying her older sister Leah first, and then permitted to marry Rachel as well.

Between them they had twelve sons, and later when God met with Jacob again in a spectacular way, He renamed him Israel. His sons later became the twelve tribes of Israel, and later again their descendants were formed into the nation of Israel.

Which of these sons would be next in line in the most important family tree in the history of the world?

Chapter 5

———— ❋ ————

*J*acob, or Israel as he must now be called, was nearing the end of his long and eventful life, so he had all of his twelve sons brought to his bedside.

"Gather around so that I can tell you what will happen to you in days to come," he said. "Assemble and listen, sons of Jacob, listen to your father Israel."

His first three sons had proved a disappointment to him, having carried out acts of which their father disapproved, so Israel turned his attention to his fourth son Judah, and through the prompting of God's Spirit, he designated the important place in the family to him.

Judah's mother Leah had given him his name, which meant "praised", because she had come to the place where she was able to praise God for this fourth son in the difficulty of her marriage as the unloved wife. Little did Leah know that this son would have the honour of being the chief of the tribe which God had chosen. Only in heaven would she understand the role that God had given her to play in His great plan of salvation. She had longed for love in her marriage, but God gave her an even greater blessing. From her son would eventually come the son of God's promise!

Israel now took up this theme of praise as he pronounced his blessing on Judah. Speaking prophetically, he blessed Judah with these words.

"Judah, your brothers will praise you:

Your hand will be on the neck of your enemies;

Your father's sons will bow down to you.

You are a lion's cub, O Judah;

You return from the prey, my son.

Like a lion he crouches and lies down, like a lioness – who dares to rouse him?

The sceptre will not depart from Judah,

Nor the ruler's staff from between his feet,

Until he comes to whom it belongs."

From henceforth the tribe of Judah was the chosen clan, and it would be from the descendants of Judah that "he" of the promise would come.

"The sceptre will not depart from Judah,

Nor the ruler's staff from between his feet,

Until he comes to whom it belongs"

Exciting words! They indicated that a king would come from Judah!

Judah was not exactly an exemplary character to begin with, having been the one to suggest that they would sell their young brother Joseph into slavery in Egypt, rather than kill him which some of his brothers suggested. They were motivated by jealousy because their father loved Joseph more than any of his other children as he was the first-born son of his beloved wife Rachel.

The story of Joseph, his coat of many colours and his astronomic rise to power in Egypt is a very familiar one, but its significance lies in how God used him to preserve the lives of his entire family during a seven year famine.

Judah rose to the occasion in the matter of Joseph's young brother Benjamin, Rachel's other son, and he offered his life as a slave to Joseph if he would permit Benjamin to return home safely to his father. He completely redeemed himself by his unselfish offer, and was genuinely repentant of his earlier cruelty, thus demonstrating that he had compassion and strength of character.

Although chosen from among the twelve sons of Jacob as the head of the family and designated as the chief clan, Judah probably did not make the best life choices, yet God chose this clan to bring about His own purposes. God would one day bring perfection out of the imperfect clan Judah.

Instead of choosing a wife from among his own people who were God-worshippers, Judah married a Canaanite woman. The narrative around Judah's marriage tells us very little, but we can assume that Judah's pagan wife brought up their three sons in her own way with little or no influence from Judah, and when they were grown up they did not embrace the faith of their father. Consequently, none of them inherited the blessing of God's promise.

Judah also chose a Canaanite bride for his eldest son Er, but Tamar, the young lady in question, clearly believed in Judah's God, and worshipped Him, forsaking her own Canaanite gods.

When her first husband died, Tamar was given in marriage to Judah's second son Onan, according to Hebrew tradition, but when he also died she was left widowed and childless. Because she believed so strongly in Judah's God she had a deep desire to remain a member of clan Judah, as was her right, but Judah sent her home to remain a widow in her father's house with a vague promise that she would be married to his third son Shelah when he was old enough.

When Shelah reached marriageable age and Judah had not approached her to arrange a marriage with him, Tamar began to wonder what she could do to assert her right to her place in Judah's family, and have a child who would be a member of clan Judah. It was her longing to belong to this family and to have a child who would also be part of this clan which motivated her to take the action which she subsequently took.

She had to wait a long time, but finally, after Judah's wife died, an opportunity arose, and Tamar grasped it. Resourceful and determined, she formed a plan, and, disguising herself as a prostitute, she sat down at the entrance to the village of Emain where she knew Judah was heading to oversee his sheep-shearing and engage in the festivities which followed.

As a result of her encounter with Judah, who had no idea that she was his daughter-in-law, Tamar gave birth to twin sons, and Judah acknowledged that she was more righteous than he, since he had not fulfilled his obligation to marry her to Shelah.

The eldest of these boys, Perez, was the next in line after his father Judah, as the progenitor of the "Lion of the Tribe of Judah", and eventually one of his descendants would bear the sceptre and the ruler's staff. That he was born from such a union is both surprising and humbling, but God, who is rich in love and mercy towards those who revere Him, frequently acts in unexpected ways. That He chose the child of Tamar as part of His plan, shows that He accepted her as belonging to the believing community, and understood her desire to worship Him and live among His people.

From now on we must follow the fortunes of Clan Judah throughout the generations until the bearer of the sceptre makes his appearance.

Four more generations pass before the next story of interest. Hezron was the son of Perez, Hezron's son was Ram, Ram's son was Amminadab and Amminadab's son was Nashon. It was Nashon's son Salmon who provided another fascinating tale which again demonstrates how often God chooses the seemingly most unlikely people to fulfill His purposes, and richly blesses them, and others through them, beyond their wildest dreams.

Chapter 6

After Israel died, his sons and their families remained in Egypt where they had come in order to escape the famine in the land of Canaan, the land God promised to give them but which they did not yet own. That time would come however because God never breaks a promise, but the time was not yet right.

At first, under the pharaoh whom Joseph knew, all was well, but later when another pharaoh ruled, he began to look askance at the Israelites, afraid that they would soon outnumber the Egyptians and turn against them, so he decided to make slaves of them, as God had predicted.

The God who cared for His people would not leave them forever at the mercy of the Egyptians, so He raised up a leader to bring them out of Egypt.

God chose Moses, an unlikely and reluctant leader at first, but in the end God met with him in spectacular ways, and conveyed to him His very own words which He instructed Moses to record for posterity.

Before their exodus from the country, God gave Moses instructions for an important ceremony which was to become a lasting ordinance. The Passover, as it was called, was deeply significant.

"Each man is to take a lamb for his family," God said.

The lamb was to be a young male without defect, and on the fourth day after selecting it they were to slaughter it. They were to take some of the blood and sprinkle it on the tops and sides of the door frames of their houses, then roast the lamb and eat it. They were to eat it in haste because that very night they would be leaving Egypt for good.

"The blood will be a sign for you on the houses where you are," God said, "and when I see the blood I will pass over you."

The Israelites would be safe if they had the blood of the lamb on their doorposts.

God was setting a pattern that would last until He sent the Lamb of God into the world. The Passover was beautifully symbolic of the One who would shed His blood for the sins of the world, the one whom God had promised.

God instructed Moses, "This is a day you are to commemorate; for the generations to come you shall celebrate it as a festival to the Lord – a lasting ordinance."

If it seems strange to us that blood should hold such significance in God's methodology, we need to remember that the shedding of blood first happened as a result of sin, and the death and destruction that followed the "fall". From henceforth God used the symbol of blood to atone for sin just as He had covered Adam and Eve with the skins of the animals whose blood He had shed.

After Moses led the Israelites out of Egypt that same night of the first Passover, they eventually came to the land God promised them. The age-old promise given to the Patriarchs was about to come to pass. God had given offspring as He had promised, and soon they would be able to call the land their own, but there still remained one aspect of the promise yet to be fulfilled, and it was to Moses that God gave the privilege of reminding the people of it.

Before they finally reached the promised land Moses gave them many important instructions which he received from God Himself as he met with Him on Mount Sinai. This was "The Law" which the Israelites were to observe, and if they did so it would ensure their well-being, and bring God's blessing upon them. If they did not keep it they would suffer the consequences.

But there was one other important piece of information which Moses conveyed to them.

Speaking prophetically Moses declared, "The Lord your God will raise up for you a prophet like me from among your brothers. You must listen to him."

Moses made it clear that "he" would come from among their own people. He reiterated what God had told him.

"The Lord said to me, 'I will raise up for them a prophet like you from among their brothers: I will put My words in his mouth, and he will tell them everything I command him.'"

Israel, directed by God, had chosen Judah from among his sons, so it is the descendants of the clan of Judah we will trace, and see how they eventually lead us to the promised one.

Chapter 7

*S*almon was the son of Nashon from the clan
of Judah. Brave, fearless and true to his God,
Salmon was a warrior in the Israelite army. When
his captain, Joshua, sent him, along with another
soldier to spy out the land of God's promise, it
turned out to be quite an adventure for Salmon.

The two young soldiers sneaked into the walled
city of Jericho and found their way to the house of
a prostitute where they were certain they would
gather some useful information. Remarkably they
discovered that the charming and resourceful
young woman whose house they had entered was
a believer in their God.

Rahab hid the spies under the flax stalks on the flat roof of her house, and when the king's men came looking for them she deliberately sent them out to the country to search for them, knowing that they would not find them since they were safe in her house.

"I know that the Lord has given you this land," Rahab told Salmon and his colleague. She continued, "The hearts of all in Jericho are melting because of you."

Rahab had heard of the God of Israel, and knew that He had performed great miracles for the Israelites. She had heard how He had dried up the waters of the Red Sea for them when they were fleeing from Egypt. She knew that their God was a God like no other, and she had abandoned her belief in the Canaanite gods her people worshipped, and had turned to the Lord God of Israel.

Declaring her faith in God she said, "The Lord your God is God in heaven above and on the earth below."

Salmon, deeply impressed by her faith in his God, was greatly encouraged by what she told them, and grateful that she was willing to hide them and not betray them to her king. They spoke together at length, and when Rahab asked them to save her entire family when they entered the city, since she had not betrayed them, they willingly agreed.

"Our lives for your lives," they assured her. "If you do not tell what we are doing, we will treat you kindly and faithfully when the Lord gives us the land."

At last, when she felt it was safe, Rahab let them down by a rope through the window, and the men escaped to the hills, eventually returning to their camp with an encouraging report for their captain, Joshua.

The day finally came when the Israelite army took Jericho, and true to their word the young soldier spies rescued Rahab and all her family. The scarlet rope which Rahab had placed on the wall of her house, showed them where she was, and like the blood on the doorposts at the Passover, it was the salvation of those within the house.

An attraction had clearly formed between the two young people, so Salmon and Rahab married and in due course had a son.

Once again God had chosen a young woman who, despite her pagan upbringing and environment, had made a conscious decision to trust in the Lord God of Israel. A prostitute from the heathen city of Jericho seemed an unlikely choice to be the mother of a son who would be an ancestor of God's promised son, but it was her faith in God and her turning away from her old life and the pagan gods of her people that pleased God. His ways are not our ways, and He knows exactly what He is doing. Often He works in unexpected ways to bring about His purposes.

It is clear too that God blessed those who turned from their pagan ways to trust in Him. And so it is today, for God does not change. He is the same God "yesterday, today and forever". He still blesses those who turn from their sin and put their trust in Him.

Salmon and Rahab named their son Boaz, and as it happened he too met and married a young foreign woman who had also come to trust in the God of Israel.

Chapter 8

———— ✳ ————

*B*oaz grew up in a home where God was honoured and worshipped, and where people of other nationalities were treated with respect.

Undoubtedly his mother Rahab had a strong influence on his life. She was a woman of courage and faith who had risked her own life in order to ensure that his father and his soldier companion were kept safe when they entered her city of Jericho.

His father too was a brave and godly man who had not been afraid to marry the girl he loved even though she was of a different race. She had openly declared her faith in his God and that was good enough for Salmon.

It is not surprising therefore that Boaz treated Ruth the Moabitess with kindness and dignity. Ruth had staunchly refused to leave Naomi, her mother-in-law when she returned to Judah from Moab where she had lost her husband and two sons.

"Where you go I will go," Ruth said to Naomi. "Your people will be my people, and your God my God."

Boaz farmed his fields outside the little town of Bethlehem in the land of Judah, and it was to his fields that Ruth came at the beginning of the barley harvest to glean barley after the reapers.

It was written into Jewish law that widows and other poor people should be allowed to glean from the fields of grain so that they could gather enough to make bread. The harvesters were to purposely leave enough around the edges of their fields for the poor so that they would not starve.

It was not long before Ruth came to the attention of Boaz, and he spoke to her kindly.

"I have been told all about what you have done for your mother-in-law since the death of your husband . . . May the Lord repay you for what you have done. May you be richly rewarded by the Lord, the God of Israel, under whose wings you have come to take refuge."

When Ruth told Naomi that she had met Boaz, Naomi told her, "He is one of our kinsman-redeemers."

In Jewish law a kinsman-redeemer was one who could buy the land from a close relative in order to keep it in the family, and he could also marry the widow of the late landowner or his son so that their names would be kept alive among the family and listed in the town records.

So Boaz bought the land that had belonged to his kinsman Elimelech, Naomi's husband, and he married Ruth, the widow of Elimelech's son, thus liberating Ruth and her much-loved mother–in-law Naomi from their poverty. It was a happy ending for all concerned! The book which bears Ruth's name recounts their heartwarming story.

Ruth and Boaz had a son whom they named Obed, and now the history of this family tree becomes exciting because Obed's son was Jesse, and Jesse's son was David! We have arrived at the first bearer of the sceptre in the clan of Judah!

Chapter 9

---※---

"*F*ill your horn with oil and be on your way," the Lord said to Samuel the prophet. "I am sending you to Jesse of Bethlehem. I have chosen one of his sons to be king."

Samuel was heart-broken over the first king of the nation of Israel. He had seemed the ideal candidate, and had started so well, but sadly Saul had not lived up to his God-given calling, and the Lord told Samuel that He had rejected him.

God instructed Samuel to hold a sacrifice at Jesse's home, so Samuel travelled to Bethlehem.

"I will show you what to do," said God. "You are to anoint for me the one I indicate."

Jesse and seven of his sons gathered for the sacrifice. Each time one of the fine looking young men passed before Samuel he thought, "Surely the Lord's anointed stands here before the Lord."

Each time the Lord showed him otherwise. He told Samuel, "Do not consider his appearance or his height, for I have rejected him. The Lord does not look at the things man looks at. Man looks at the outward appearance, but the Lord looks at the heart."

After all seven of Jesse's sons had passed in front of Samuel, and the Lord had made it clear that He had not chosen any of them, Samuel asked Jesse, "Are these all the sons you have?"

"There is still the youngest," replied Jesse, "but he is tending the sheep."

"Send for him," said Samuel. "We will not sit down until he arrives."

Samuel must have known even before David came in that he was the one God had chosen because he was the last of Jesse's sons, and he was not disappointed when he saw him. Although he was handsome looking like his brothers, there was something more to David than his fine appearance. The goodness in David's heart and his devotion to his God was shining in his eyes, and Samuel's ear was attuned to hear what God would say.

"Rise and anoint him; he is the one," said God.

There in the presence of his older brothers, young David was anointed with oil, and from that day on God's Spirit came upon him in power.

Once again God had chosen the least likely candidate to fulfill His purpose; the least likely to human eyes, but God looks into the heart, and bases His choice on what He sees there. In David He saw a man who would put Him first and carry out His will, a man capable of leading a nation to greatness and one who would keep them true to their God.

It would be a long time before David could take his place as king, and he had many trials to endure before then, but he was God's choice, God's anointed and "a man after God's own heart."

As long as Saul remained king, David could not claim his right to the throne, so he went back to his sheep and waited, and as he waited he played his harp, composed exquisite poetry and communed with his God.

The Spirit of God had departed from Saul because he had failed to do as God commanded, and he began to become depressed and unstable. His servants could see that he needed healing for his inner emotional and spiritual turmoil, so they suggested bringing a harpist to him to calm him and restore his spirits. Saul liked the idea so he instructed his servants to find someone for him.

Who should it be but David! The king's servant described David perfectly to Saul.

"I have seen a son of Jesse who knows how to play a harp. He is a brave man and a warrior. He speaks well and is a fine-looking man. And the Lord is with him."

"The Lord is with him." This phrase characterized David right from the beginning and throughout his life. He loved the Lord his God and sought to serve Him faithfully.

David's beautiful music soothed Saul's troubled soul, and his pleasing personality appealed to him, so he invited David to become his armour-bearer. By night David continued to play for Saul, and by day he went out with Saul's army.

Everyone knows the story of David and Goliath, and what a wonderful story it is–the arrogant Philistine giant taunting the indignant young Israeli warrior!

In response to his threats David declared confidently, "I come against you in the name of the Lord Almighty, the God of the armies of Israel whom you have defied."

Taking his sling and his stones David approached him unhesitatingly, declaring, "This day the Lord will hand you over to me."

The stone hit Goliath between the eyes and the fight was over before it had begun. At once the Philistines fled with the Israelite army in hot pursuit, and the day saw great deliverance for Israel.

David's mighty exploit had far-reaching repercussions. Saul gave him a high rank in the army, and David fought so successfully that he earned a considerable reputation for himself.

As the army returned from battle, the women would go out singing and dancing to welcome them back.

"Saul has slain his thousands, and David his tens of thousands," they sang.

This evoked great jealousy in Saul's heart, and from henceforth he saw David as his enemy. Over the following years Saul sought to kill David, and as he fled from place to place, often sheltering in mountain caves or even in hostile neighbouring countries, David grew tired of the endless running from Saul. Yet these were the times when he composed some of his most emotive and striking poetry as he poured out his soul to his God.

"Be merciful to me O God, for men hotly pursue me;

All day long they press their attack . . .

All day long they twist my words;

They are always plotting to harm me.

They conspire, they lurk, they watch my steps, eager to take my life."

Often David must have felt close to death as Saul's men closed in on him, but always he knew that his God was watching over him, and he was able to say, "When I am afraid I will trust in You."

Whether he was in a cave or in the fields outside Bethlehem, David drew on the deep relationship he had with God, and constantly reminded himself of God's love and mercy.

"Great is your love, reaching to the heavens;

Your faithfulness reaches to the skies."

The best known of all David's beautiful songs was written when he was hiding from Saul in a deep cave at Engedi in the rocky desert area of Judah. At that time his life was lonely and distressing, devoid of any material comforts, but his words paint a peaceful picture of a gentle pastoral scene reminiscent of his early life when he was tending his father's sheep.

"The Lord is my shepherd, I shall not be in want.

He makes me lie down in green pastures,

He leads me beside quiet waters,

He restores my soul."

The lovely words have brought comfort to thousands of lonely troubled souls since David first composed them around three thousand years ago.

"Even though I walk through the valley of the shadow of death,

I will fear no evil, for you are with me."

David often found himself in the valley of the shadow, but God provided the strength and comfort, and although deeply distressed and saddened that Saul considered him an enemy, David was unafraid.

"Surely goodness and mercy will follow me

All the days of my life,

And I will dwell in the house of the Lord forever."

During all his years of adversity when he was forced to flee from Saul, David was constantly thrown back on God for the help and protection he needed. From the depths of his anguished soul he cried out to God in prayer, and his heart-felt pleas have resonated with countless others who have found themselves in dark and desperate circumstances.

"Listen to my prayer, O God, do not ignore my plea; hear me and answer me.

My thoughts trouble me and I am distraught at the voice of the enemy . . .

My heart is in anguish within me; the terrors of death assail me."

God did not disappoint him, and David acknowledged His faithfulness as He protected him and strengthened him.

"I love you O Lord my strength.

The Lord is my rock, my fortress and my deliverer.

My God is my rock in whom I take refuge.

He is my shield and the horn of my salvation, my stronghold.

I call to the Lord who is worthy of praise, and I am saved from my enemies."

David was a man devoted to his God, and his God was loving and faithful. He was also compassionate, merciful and forgiving as David would later discover.

Chapter 10

$\mathcal{A}$t last the time came when David's fugitive days were over and he was able to return to normal life. King Saul had been killed in battle, so God directed David to go to Hebron in the territory of Judah, where the people of clan Judah welcomed him as their king.

The ten tribes who were loyal to Saul chose Ish-Bosheth, of the house of Saul, as their king, but eventually when they began to experience problems they decided to ask David to be their king.

"We are your own flesh and blood. In the past, while Saul was king over us, you were the one who led Israel on their military campaigns. And the

Lord said to you, 'You shall shepherd my people Israel, and you shall become their ruler.'"

They recognized David's leadership qualities, and they acknowledged that God had chosen him, so David was crowned king over all twelve tribes of Israel, and he set up his throne in Jerusalem which became the capital city. A beautiful palace of cedar wood was built for him and life began to be much more comfortable for David.

Since he now had a permanent home of his own it was David's great desire to build a house for the Lord, a place for the Ark of God's Presence which had finally been brought up to Jerusalem. He confided in Nathan the prophet that this was his wish, and a little later, when God had spoken to Nathan, he came to see David.

"Go and tell my servant David, 'This is what the Lord says'," began Nathan.

God made wonderful promises to David just as He had done with his ancestors.

"The Lord declares to you that the Lord Himself will establish a house for you," Nathan told him. "I will raise up your offspring to succeed you, who will come from your own body, and I will establish his kingdom. He is the one who will build a house for my Name, and I will establish the throne of his kingdom for ever."

When Nathan had imparted God's entire revelation to David, he concluded with God's own words, "'Your house and your kingdom shall endure for ever before me; your throne shall be established for ever.'"

David was overcome with God's goodness, and stirred with deep emotion, he went and sat before the Lord.

"Who am I, O Sovereign Lord," he said humbly, "and what is my family, that you have brought me thus far? And as if this were not enough in your sight, O Sovereign Lord, you have also spoken about the future of the house of your servant."

God's amazing generosity to David evoked a sense of profound worship in him, and he expressed his deep gratitude to God as well as his acute awareness of the majesty of God.

"How great you are O Sovereign Lord! There is no-one like you, and there is no God but you."

The final words of his prayer acknowledged the sovereignty of God who would so graciously bring His word to pass because He is an unchanging God who fulfills what He promises.

"O Sovereign Lord, you are God! Your words are trustworthy, and you have promised these good things to your servant. Now be pleased to bless the house of your servant, that it may continue for ever in your sight; for you O Sovereign Lord have spoken, and with your blessing the house of your servant will be blessed for ever."

There is little that any king would want more than a son who would succeed him, and when God made this promise to David it is no wonder he sat enthralled in the presence of God. To be blessed for ever with dynastic succession was almost too wonderful to take in, but the Sovereign Lord had spoken and David poured out his humble thanks to God for such a blessing.

It was customary among eastern kings at that time to have several wives as they needed many sons in order to keep their kingdoms strong and ensure dynastic succession, and David was no exception. He already had six wives when he moved his court from Hebron up to Jerusalem. Some of them were marriages of conveniences or political alliances, but when he met Bathsheba he met the love of his life.

Bathsheba was a very beautiful woman, the daughter of Eliab, one of David's special elite force of warriors. They were known as his mighty men, and Eliab was a member of the tribe of Judah, David's own clan.

Surprising though it may be, Eliab did not arrange a marriage for his daughter with a man of Judah. Instead he married her to a Hittite which was one of the nations with whom the Israelites were not to intermarry as they worshipped false gods.

The Biblical record does not tells us whether Uriah, Bathsheba's husband, was a God-worshipper or not, but we gather that he was an honourable man, and he too was one of David's mighty men, a skilled, dedicated and courageous soldier.

When David first set eyes on Bathsheba she was bathing in a little pool in the courtyard of her home, not far from David's palace. As he observed her from the roof of his palace and saw how beautiful she was he sent messengers to bring her to him.

David had been a good and godly man all his life up to this point, but as we can glean from the Biblical text, he fell instantly in love with Bathsheba, and on this occasion impulsively yielded to his feelings which sadly led him to commit adultery.

No-one can sin with impunity, and there were bitter consequences to David's action. When Bathsheba sent word to him that she was with child he tried in vain to rectify the situation, but in the end he occasioned the death of Uriah by sending him into the thick of a battle where he knew he would be killed, and the way was then clear for him to marry Bathsheba.

The Lord sent Nathan the prophet to David to tell him how deeply displeased He was with his actions. God reminded him how much He had done for him in delivering him from Saul and anointing him king over Israel.

In words of strong rebuke God said, "Why did you despise the word of the Lord by doing what is evil in his eyes?"

Deeply convicted, David humbly confessed, "I have sinned against the Lord."

"The Lord has taken away your sin," Nathan told him. "You are not going to die. But because by doing this you have made the enemies of the Lord show utter contempt, the son born to you will die."

When the little son of David and Bathsheba was seven days old he died. David was deeply saddened, but he acknowledged the sovereignty of God and spoke true and strangely comforting words.

"I will go to him, but he will not return to me."

David knew he would go to be with his little baby in heaven one day, and as he sat before the

Lord in repentance the words of his prayer express the depths of his contrition.

"Have mercy on me, O God, according to your unfailing love;

According to your great compassion blot out my transgressions.

Wash away all my iniquity and cleanse me from my sin . . .

Against you, you only, have I sinned and done what is evil in your sight . . .

Save me from bloodguilt, O God, the God who saves me."

David remembered that when Saul disobeyed God the Lord took His Spirit from him, and David pleaded with God that He would not do the same with him.

"Create in me a pure heart, O God, and renew a steadfast spirit within me.

Do not cast me off from your presence or take your Holy Spirit from me.

Restore to me the joy of your salvation and grant me a willing spirit to sustain me."

David's repentance was genuine and as he experienced God's gracious forgiveness he expressed his heartfelt gratitude in another beautiful song of praise.

"Praise the Lord, O my soul, and forget not all his benefits –

Who forgives all your sins and heals all your diseases . . .

The Lord is compassionate and gracious, slow to anger, abounding in love.

He does not always accuse, nor will he harbour his anger for ever;

He does not treat us as our sins deserve, or repay us according to our iniquities.

For as high as the heavens are above the earth,

So great is his love for those who fear him;

As far as the east is from the west,

So far has he removed our transgressions from us."

In due course David and Bathsheba had another son, and this was the son whom God chose to fulfill His promise to David when He said, "I will raise up your offspring to succeed you, who will come from your own body, and I will establish his kingdom."

Although David already had six sons by his six previous wives, the eldest son of Bathsheba was the one God chose to succeed his father. The Biblical record tells us that "the Lord loved him" and although he was not David's eldest son he was the one of God's choice, just as David was God's choice, although the youngest of his family.

It was as if David and Bathsheba were always meant to be together as husband and wife. Interestingly, Bathsheba's name means 'daughter of promise', and perhaps it could even be translated 'daughter of *the* promise', which would make her marriage to David deeply significant; the bearer of the sceptre married to the daughter of the promise! Later they had three more sons, the next one whom they named Nathan out of regard for their good friend the prophet of the Lord. Nathan too had an important role to play in the history of clan Judah, as we will later see.

Chapter 11

―――― ✳ ――――

*D*avid's Psalms are full of passion, prayer and praise, but many of them are also prophetic. David was God's chosen son of Judah to bear the sceptre, but he was also God's chosen mouthpiece to proclaim His word to future generations. When Samuel took the horn of oil and anointed David, "from that day on the Spirit of the Lord came upon David in power." It was the Spirit of God who inspired David to write prophetic words.

David lived around 1000 years before the coming of God's Anointed One, the Messiah, the "he" of the promise, but he wrote so accurately about some of the events surrounding him that it is certain the words were inspired by God's Spirit.

When the time came, those who were familiar with David's Psalms recognized that his words were indeed prophetic.

In Psalm 2 David wrote, "The kings of the earth take their stand, and the rulers gather together against the Lord and against His Anointed One." Later it became clear that this referred to those who opposed God's Anointed whom He sent in fulfillment of His promise.

"I have installed my King on Zion, my holy hill," declared the Lord. It would be in the future but David wrote about it in his lifetime, centuries before it happened.

Psalm 22 is a powerful and graphic description of what it would be like for God's Anointed One to endure the scorn and pain of those who would put him to death.

"I am a worm and not a man,
 Scorned by men and despised by the people.
 All who see me mock me;
 They hurl insults, shaking their heads:
 He trusts in the Lord;

Let the Lord rescue him.

Let Him deliver him,

Since he delights in him."

These prophetic words, full of pathos, would become a reality when the time came.

"I am poured out like water,

And all my bones are out of joint. . . .

My strength is dried up like a potsherd,

And my tongue sticks to the roof of my mouth;

You lay me in the dust of death.

Dogs have surrounded me; a band of evil men has encircled me,

They have pierced my hands and my feet.

I can count all my bones;

People stare and gloat over me.

They divide my garments among them, and cast lots for my clothing."

David paints a vivid picture of the suffering of God's Anointed One enduring the pain of death by crucifixion. The description is so accurate that it is impossible to relate it to anything else, and it certainly does not refer to David himself, for although his enemies ceaselessly pursued him, the words do not apply to his experience.

Although God's Anointed would be put to death he would not remain in the grave, and the Spirit of God reveals this to David. Psalm 16 records his prophetic words.

"Therefore my heart is glad and my tongue rejoices;

My body also will rest secure,

Because you will not abandon me to the grave,

Nor will you let your Holy One see decay."

Clearly David was not writing about himself, because Biblical history records that "David rested with his fathers and was buried in the City of David."

The closing words of the Psalm go further, assuring us that God's Holy One will, after his resurrection, go into the presence of God to sit at His right hand.

"You will fill me with joy in your presence,

With eternal pleasures at your right hand."

There is a line in Psalm 72 which bears a striking similarity to the promise God gave to the patriarchs, Abraham, Isaac and Jacob: "All nations will be blessed through him, and they will call him blessed."

Although this psalm is entitled "Of Solomon" it is possible that David wrote it for Solomon his son, looking ahead to the time when he would succeed him on the throne, and it is also Messianic in nature, as much of it indicates.

"Endow the king with your justice, O God, the royal son with your righteousness. . .

He will endure as long as the sun, as long as the moon,

Through all generations . . .

All nations will be blessed through him, and they will call him blessed."

David's writings are full of prophetic statements. God's Spirit powerfully spoke through him to let future generations know that He had a plan, not only for Judah and Israel but also for the whole world, and that He would bring His plan to fulfillment in His time and in His way.

Chapter 12

———— ❋ ————

"*I* saw the Lord, seated on a throne, high and exalted."

Isaiah was awed by the majesty and holiness of Almighty God who he saw in his vision, and overwhelmed by his own sinfulness.

"Woe to me!" he cried. "I am a man of unclean lips, and I live among a people of unclean lips, and my eyes have seen the King, the Lord Almighty."

One of the seraphs who surrounded God's throne touched his lips with a live coal from the altar, and this act signified his cleansing.

"Your guilt is taken away and your sin is atoned for," the seraph told him.

After this Isaiah heard the voice of God asking, "Whom shall I send? And who will go for us?"

Instantly Isaiah willingly replied, "Here am I. Send me."

So God commissioned Isaiah to go out among the people of Judah and preach. His message was a mixture of dire warnings and great encouragement with much of it containing predictions which pertained to the future. It was through the prophets that God spoke to His people, and it was through them that He gave wonderful prophecies concerning the promised Saviour.

Isaiah lived during the reigns of several of King David's descendants. David had built a strong kingdom, uniting the kingdom of Judah (which also included the small tribe of Benjamin) and the other ten tribes, into the nation of Israel. His son Solomon had inherited a peaceful united nation, and while he ruled it remained so, but sadly, at the end of his reign he permitted, and even engaged in worship to false gods to please his foreign wives of whom he had many.

"As Solomon grew old, his wives turned his heart after other gods, and his heart was not fully devoted to the Lord his God, as the heart of David his father had been."

This was contrary to God's command. God had issued specific instructions to the people through Moses. When they entered the land that God promised to them they were warned not to intermarry with other nations or follow their practices.

"The king," warned Moses, "must not take many wives, or his heart will be led astray."

Sadly this is exactly what happened, and it was for this reason that God sent his prophets to preach to the people and remind them of God's laws, given to them through Moses.

Furthermore, Moses had said, "The king is to write for himself on a scroll a copy of this law. It is to be with him, and he is to read it, all the days of his life so that he may learn to revere the Lord his God and follow carefully all the words of this law and these decrees."

God expected His people to keep His Law which He gave them for their well-being. Indeed He expects the same from us. David expressed it so well in another lovely Psalm. (Ps 19).

"The law of the Lord is perfect, reviving the soul.

The statutes of the Lord are trustworthy, making wise the simple.

The precepts of the Lord are right, giving joy to the heart.

The commands of the Lord are radiant, giving light to the eyes...

They are more precious than gold, than much pure gold;

By them is your servant warned; in keeping them there is great reward."

Moses had outlined the blessing which would come from keeping God's Law, but also the disaster if they failed to keep it, and the king was no different, in fact as leader of the people it was up to him to set an example. Moses declared that if the king kept God's Law, "he and his descendants will reign a long time over his kingdom in Israel."

In spite of all God had done for Solomon, giving him riches beyond measure as well as the gifts of wisdom and knowledge, and in addition great fame among nations far beyond Israel's borders, Solomon disappointed God, and God told him He would wrest his kingdom from him.

A faithful, unchanging God would not break His promise to David, so He told Solomon, "For the sake of David your father, I will not do it during your lifetime. I will tear it out of the hand of your son. Yet I will not tear the whole kingdom from him, but will give him one tribe for the sake of David my servant, and for the sake of Jerusalem which I have chosen."

When he succeeded to the throne Rehoboam, Solomon's son, treated his subjects harshly, so they rebelled against him and chose instead Jeroboam, a former official of Solomon, an able young man of considerable standing. They made him king over the ten tribes of Israel while Rehoboam, David's grandson, retained his rule over Judah, just as God had decreed.

The record of the kings who succeeded Rehoboam makes sad and sombre reading as many of them continued to reject God's law and engage in evil practices.

When Isaiah began to preach he warned them that they would suffer the consequences of their sin if they did not repent. As always God gave His people a chance to turn from their sin and return to Him. If they did he would forgive them since He was a gracious and merciful God, but if they continued to reject Him and go on in their sinful ways, there would be consequences as He had warned them already through Moses.

King Ahaz was the ninth king from David, and the first king of Judah Isaiah approached with God's message. Judah was about to be invaded by two neighbouring kings, and God sent Isaiah to bring an encouraging message to King Ahaz.

"It will not take place, it will not happen," Isaiah told him.

Ahaz took no comfort from this, not being a true worshipper of the Lord, and he was busy making other plans to obtain help from elsewhere.

"If you do not stand firm in your faith you will not stand at all," warned Isaiah.

What a timely word! Faith in God was what was needed, but in spite of all that God had done for His people in the past, and was willing to do for them in the present, Ahaz was still trusting in his own strength and that of others instead of relying on God's word.

God spoke to Ahaz again through Isaiah.

"Ask the Lord your God for a sign," he said, but Ahaz refused.

"The Lord Himself will give you a sign," Isaiah told him. "The virgin will be with child and will give birth to a son, and will call him Immanuel."

Immanuel, God with us! What amazing encouragement!

The prophecy was not just for Ahaz at that time, although it was meant to encourage him to trust in the help of God in his circumstances. It was, in fact, a prophecy concerning the promised Saviour! Other words, relevant to Ahaz's particular situation were also spoken, but Ahaz did not believe any of it, so Isaiah warned him that Assyria, a much greater enemy than he presently faced, would come and lay waste to the land, taking the inhabitants into captivity in Babylon.

Often Isaiah's prophecies were like rolling hills which stretched away into the distance. Close hills zoomed in to the present situation, farther hills represented future events, distant hills concerned events which would only come to pass in the far distant future, and the faint blue mountains barely visible against the horizon were the ultimate end of God's prophetic word.

Isaiah's central message warned that Judah would be taken into captivity, but that it would not be for ever. God would be gracious and He would fulfill His purpose for His people and bring final deliverance.

As well as warnings Isaiah brought many joyous predictions, not only to the people of Judah but to the whole world. God had promised that all nations on earth would be blessed through the coming of His Anointed One.

"There will be no more gloom for the people in distress," Isaiah foretold. "He [God] will honour Galilee of the Gentiles, by the way of the sea, along the Jordan – The people walking in darkness have seen a great light; on those living in the land of the shadow of death a light has dawned."

This was very specific! He would come to the area of Galilee in northern Israel.

Later Isaiah proclaimed again, "See, darkness covers the earth and thick darkness is over the people, but the Lord rises upon you, and His glory appears over you."

Looking ahead to the One who would come to bring light and salvation, Isaiah declared, "Nations will come to your light and kings to the brightness of your dawn."

The dawn of which he spoke was the birth of the promised Saviour.

"For to us a child is born, to us a son is given, and the government will be upon his shoulders. And he will be called Wonderful, Counsellor, Mighty God, Everlasting Father, Prince of Peace."

What an astounding prophecy! What did it mean? Well, God had given His clearest indication yet as to the real identity of the Saviour! He would come from God Himself!

This draws together the humanity and the deity of the Anointed One. He would descend from David in his humanity according to God's promise, but he would also be divine. To us that is a mystery! Only God could devise such a plan.

Isaiah continued, "Of the increase of his government and peace there will be no end. He will reign on David's throne and over his kingdom establishing it and upholding it with justice and righteousness from that time on and for ever."

Isaiah had the near hills and the far distant mountains in view again. The Saviour would come, born of the virgin. He would be the Prince of Peace for all who desired his peace, but ultimately he would be King of Kings and Lord of Lords when all the nations would worship at his feet, and he would rule with justice and righteousness.

The kings of Israel and Judah had failed to rule in righteousness so they would be taken into captivity and exile, but there was hope and comfort, Isaiah assured them. It would come first in their return from exile, but greater comfort, light and salvation was to come.

"A shoot will come up from the stump of Jesse; from his roots a Branch will bear fruit. The Spirit of the Lord will rest on him – the Spirit of wisdom and understanding, the Spirit of counsel and of power, the Spirit of knowledge and of the fear of the Lord."

The kings of Judah had lost their standing and their power. They would not regain it when they returned from captivity. Their only hope was in the Branch that would spring from the stump of Jesse. Their king would descend from David as God had promised, but he would be so much greater than David.

In beautiful poetic language Isaiah joyously proclaimed, "A voice of one calling: In the desert prepare the way for the Lord, make straight in the wilderness a highway for our God. Every valley shall be raised up, every mountain and hill made low; . . . and the glory of the Lord will be revealed, and all mankind together will see it. For the mouth of the Lord has spoken."

It was a thrilling message, and Isaiah knew that God had given it, not just for Judah but for the whole world.

"You who bring good tidings to Zion . . . say to the cities of Judah, 'Here is your God!'"

Their God would come to bring salvation as He had promised. It was good news!

"How beautiful upon the mountains are the feet of those who bring good news, who proclaim peace, who bring good tidings, who proclaim salvation, who say to Zion 'Your God reigns!'"

There are many beautiful expression of God's kindness and encouragement which are intended, not just for the people of Isaiah's day, but also for a later age, as well as for us today.

"Burst into songs of joy together, you ruins of Jerusalem,

For the Lord has comforted his people, he has redeemed Jerusalem,

The Lord will lay bare his holy arm in the sight of all the nations,

And all the ends of the earth will see the salvation of our God."

It confirms God's promise that all nations will be blessed through the Saviour.

"Here is my servant, whom I uphold. My chosen One in whom I delight; I will put my Spirit on him and he will bring justice to the nations."

There is so much injustice in the world. Surely this word is of great comfort! The time when God's chosen One will bring justice to the nations is still to come, and when Isaiah was inspired to speak these words there was still much to take place before the faint smoky blue mountains of the distant horizon would bring in God's final reign and rule over all the earth.

Chapter 13

One of the most heartrending and poignant passages which Isaiah penned describes the suffering of the One whom God would send into the world as Saviour in fulfillment of His word.

Firstly, Isaiah introduces him: "He grew up before him like a tender shoot, and like a root out of dry ground."

The virgin of whom Isaiah had already spoken would give birth to a son, and he would grow up as a root sprung from Jesse, a tender shoot from the house of David. This would fulfill God's promise to David that his house and his kingdom would be established for ever, but it would be at a time when conditions were not favourable for such growth because Judah would be taken over by others. Nevertheless, God would bring it about in His own appointed time.

"See, my servant will act wisely; he will be raised and lifted up and highly exalted. Just as there were many who were appalled at him – his appearance was so disfigured beyond that of any man and his form marred beyond human likeness."

He is described as God's servant and he would fulfill God's will and purpose.

"I offered my back to those who struck me, my cheeks to those who pulled out my beard."

God knew what lay ahead for His promised Saviour. He gave Isaiah prophetic insight into this distant event and Isaiah expressed it in words of deep pathos. There is profound sorrow in the prophecy, sorrow for Isaiah as he wrote it, and sorrow for the Saviour as he would endure it.

"He was despised and rejected by men, a man of sorrows, and familiar with suffering."

Isaiah predicted how he would be treated. In words reminiscent of David's prophecy in Psalm

2, he would be rejected by the rulers and leaders of the people he came to save.

"He was pierced for our transgressions, he was crushed for our iniquities, the punishment that brought us peace was upon him, and by his wounds we are healed."

To the one who would bring justice to the nations, appalling injustice would be shown – he would be despised, rejected, pierced, crushed, wounded. For Israel! For us! For our peace, our healing, our salvation. What amazing love!

Centuries before it took place Isaiah wrote about it.

"He was oppressed and afflicted, yet he did not open his mouth; he was led like a lamb to the slaughter, and as a sheep before her shearers is silent, so he did not open his mouth."

He would be the Lamb who would atone for sin. He would give his life, not only for Judah and Israel but for all of us. There would be no more need for lambs to be sacrificed for sin. He would be the perfect sacrifice!

"He poured out his life unto death, and was numbered with the transgressors. For he bore the sin of many, and made intercession for the transgressors."

For us! So that we could have our sin forgiven. He would be the Saviour!

These words indicate that, sinless though he was, he would die along with sinners, and strangely, his grave would be with the rich. But the grave could not hold him, for although "it was the Lord's will to crush him and cause him to suffer, and though the Lord makes his life a guilt offering", he would return from the darkness of the grave.

"After the suffering of his soul, he will see the light of life and be satisfied."

The words were similar to David's when he said God would not permit His Holy One to see decay. When he had fulfilled God's purpose of salvation he would arise from the grave, and return to be with God.

"My righteous servant will justify many," God said.

He had promised that all nations would be blessed through him.

Although there was sorrow associated with the coming of the Anointed One, there was also joy. Isaiah brought such encouragement to Judah.

"The Lord has made proclamation to the ends of the earth: 'Say to the Daughter of Zion, See your Saviour comes!'"

This was wonderful news! The long promised Saviour would come, and when he came he would minister to the people of Judah and Israel.

"The Spirit of the Sovereign Lord is upon me, because the Lord has anointed me to preach good news to the poor. He has sent me to bind up the broken-hearted, to proclaim freedom for the captives and release from darkness for the prisoners."

Judah would experience the blessings the Saviour would bring, as would the whole world, but looking beyond to the far distant horizon Isaiah gives God's ultimate word.

"From one New Moon to another and from one Sabbath to another, all mankind will come and bow down before Me, says the Lord."

God had spoken!

Chapter 14

The prophet Jeremiah prophesied during the reigns of three of King David's successors – Josiah, who was a good king, Jehoiakim who was not, and Zedekiah who was the last reigning king of Judah when the little nation was carried off to captivity in Babylon.

God had spoken to Jeremiah and anointed him for His service just as He had done with Isaiah.

"Before you were born I set you apart; I appointed you as a prophet to the nations," God said.

Somewhat reluctant, Jeremiah responded, "Ah Sovereign Lord, I do not know how to speak. I am only a child."

God had specifically chosen Jeremiah so He was not interested in hearing any excuses.

"Do not say, 'I am only a child,'" said God. "You must go to everyone I send you to and say whatever I command you."

Then God graciously touched Jeremiah's mouth and told him, "Now I have put my words in your mouth. See, today I appoint you over nations and kingdoms to uproot and tear down, to destroy and overthrow, to build and to plant."

Jeremiah quickly realized what a privilege God had given him, young as he was, to become His mouthpiece as a prophet to the nations, so he accepted his calling and made himself ready to take God's word to the people.

Prophets were forthtellers as much as foretellers and Jeremiah's God-given task was to preach to the people of Judah. The ten tribes of Israel had already been taken into exile in Assyria, and the same fate awaited Judah if she did not forsake her sin and return to the Lord.

God, who cared deeply about His people warned Judah constantly through Jeremiah. He told Jeremiah to go and stand at the gate of the Temple and proclaim His message.

"This is what the Lord Almighty, the God of Israel says: Will you steal and murder, commit adultery and perjury, burn incense to Baal and follow other gods you have not known, and then come and stand before me in this house, which bears my Name, and say, "We are safe" – safe to do all these detestable things? Has this house which bears my Name, become a den of robbers to you? But I have been watching!' declares the Lord.'"

In strongly emotive words God pleaded with His beloved people.

"Speak this word to them," He told Jeremiah. "'Let my eyes overflow with tears night and day without ceasing; for my virgin daughter – my people – has suffered a grievous wound, a crushing blow.'"

The words predicted what would happen to Judah, and clearly it distressed God deeply. He longed that they would forsake their sin and the false gods they worshipped. He warned them, "Look, an army is coming from the land of the north .. to attack you, O Daughter of Zion."

Tragically Judah did not heed the word of God which came from the lips of Jeremiah, and it would only be a matter of time before disaster would overtake them.

Looking ahead with prophetic insight Jeremiah questioned, "Why has the land been ruined and laid waste like a desert that no-one can cross?" and the answer came from the Lord, "It is because they have forsaken my law which I set before them."

All the warnings went unheeded as the day of their destiny drew nearer, but God had made promises to the nation of Judah which He would not break, so interspersed among the warnings were prophetic words of comfort which would encourage Judah in the future.

"The days are coming," declared the Lord, "when I will raise up to David a righteous Branch, a King who will reign wisely and do what is just and right in the land. In his days Judah will be saved and

Israel will live in safety. This is the name by which he will be called: The Lord Our Righteousness."

This gracious prophecy looked ahead to the Branch. Isaiah had spoken of the Branch, and now God gave the same prophetic words to Jeremiah. As in the earlier time when Isaiah preached, so now God encouraged the people of Jeremiah's time that a righteous Branch would grow from the root of David. In other words a wise and righteous King would spring from David's royal line, and he would be no ordinary king. He would be The Lord our Righteousness!

God is so gracious, so faithful, so merciful! Though Judah and Israel had rejected Him and become so wicked that He would allow them to be taken into captivity, He consistently reassured them that He would not forsake them, but would keep the promises He made and provide the Saviour whom He had promised from the very beginning of their history.

God repeated His words of encouragement and comfort to Judah.

"The days are coming," declares the Lord, "when I will fulfill the gracious promise I made to the house of Israel and to the house of Judah."

God repeated His words of encouragement and comfort to Judah.

"In those days and at that time I will make a righteous Branch sprout from David's line; he will do what is just and right in the land. In those days Judah will be saved and Jerusalem will live in safety. This is the name by which he will be called: The Lord Our Righteousness."

God reiterated His promise to David: "For this is what the Lord says: 'David will never fail to have a man to sit on the throne of the house of Israel.'"

God had made His pronouncement and His promise. Judah would suffer captivity, would return, would be restored, and the Righteous Branch would appear – close hills, farther hills and distant hills.

What God says comes to pass!

Chapter 15

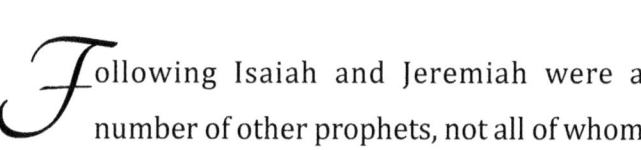

$\mathcal{F}$ollowing Isaiah and Jeremiah were a number of other prophets, not all of whom spoke of the coming Saviour, though all of them had something important to say.

Some are better known than others – Ezekiel and the valley of dry bones, Daniel and his startling visions, Jonah and the whale, Hosea and his unfaithful wife, Joel and the army of locusts. These strange and unusual allegories serve to highlight a particular aspect of their experience.

Ezekiel, Daniel and Hosea were a little later than Jeremiah, Joel a little earlier while Jonah was the earliest of all the prophets, and since he had nothing to say regarding the promised Saviour he needs only a brief mention.

The moral of the story of Jonah is that God is concerned about everyone in His world, even the people in the wicked city of Ninevah which is why He sent Jonah to preach to them. Although Jonah was not at all concerned about Ninevah, he did make one striking statement.

"Those who cling to worthless idols forfeit the grace that could be theirs."

Joel writes of "the day of the Lord" which is coming. He speaks figuratively of an invasion of locusts and warns the people of Judah that "a large and mighty army comes" unless they return to the Lord. The warnings are mixed with mercy because "the Lord will be jealous for his land and take pity on his people," and promises, "I will repay you for the years the locusts have eaten."

God shows Himself to be a merciful God and He tells His people, "I will pour out my Spirit in those days . . . before the coming of the great and dreadful day of the Lord. And everyone who calls on the name of the Lord will be saved."

This prophetic word was not just for Israel. It was meant for us too.

The prophet Hosea was given a very striking and important prophecy, part of which has already come to pass, and part of which is still future.

"For the Israelites will live for many days without king or prince, without sacrifice or sacred stones, without ephod or idol. Afterwards the Israelites will return and seek the Lord their God and David their king. They will come trembling to the Lord and to his blessings in the last days."

As we know the Israelis have no king or prince, but in the "last days" they will acknowledge the Lord their God and David their king when he comes to reign.

The prophet Obadiah declared the word of the Lord: "The day of the Lord is near for all nations . . . But on Mount Zion will be deliverance; it will be holy, and the house of Jacob will inherit its inheritance."

Zephaniah had a lovely comforting word for Judah: "The Lord your God is with you, he is mighty to save. He will take great delight in you, he will quiet you with his love, he will rejoice over you with singing."

Nahum declared, "Look, there on the mountains, the feet of one who brings good news, who proclaims peace."

On the same theme, Malachi prophesied, "'See I will send my messenger, who will prepare the way before me. Then suddenly the Lord you are seeking will come to his temple; the messenger of the covenant whom you desire, will come,'" says the Lord Almighty."

Malachi gives another word of great solace: "But for you who revere my name, the sun of righteousness will rise with healing in its wings."

In a similar theme Haggai declares the word of the Lord: "I will shake all nations and the desired of all nations will come, and I will fill this house with glory."

The prophet Amos refers to David, the king who would come.

"In that day I will restore David's fallen tent. I will repair its broken places, restore its ruins and build it as it used to be."

And Habakkuk speaks of the end times when God and His king will reign supreme.

"For the earth will be filled with the knowledge of the glory of the Lord as the waters cover the sea."

The messenger who will prepare the way for the Lord is predicted, David's descendant the Saviour is promised, and the future rule of God and His king, is promised by these prophets.

Such prophecies give supreme comfort to everyone.

Chapter 16

The prophet Ezekiel was already in exile in Babylonia along with King Jehoichin and the first group of people from Jerusalem who had been taken captive from Judah. It was Ezekiel's God-given task to preach to this group who had suffered the horrors and indignity of captivity, and who longed to return to Jerusalem.

Ezekiel too, like Isaiah and Jeremiah, had a vision of the glory of God as he beheld Him among the strange-looking living creatures who surrounded Him. It was a glorious vision with brilliant light surrounding God who sat on a throne of sapphire.

Ezekiel described the scene in beautifully poetic language: "Like the appearance of a rainbow in the clouds on a rainy day, so was the radiance around him."

As with Isaiah whose mouth was touched with a live coal from the altar, and Jeremiah whose mouth God filled with His word, so Ezekiel was given a little scroll to eat, symbolizing God's word.

God told him to go to his countrymen and speak His words to them.

"Repent! Turn away from all your offences; then sin will not be your downfall. Rid yourselves of all the offences you have committed, and get a new heart and a new spirit. Why will you die, O house of Israel? For I take no pleasure in the death of anyone, declares the Sovereign Lord. Repent and live!"

Ezekiel went to the elders of Judah where they were living in exile in Babylon. They were filled with deep longing to return to Jerusalem but Ezekiel showed them that first of all they must return to their God. With many signs, symbols and words of warning Ezekiel told them how the glory of the Lord would depart from the Temple, the city would be ruined, and those who escaped the sword would be carried into captivity as they themselves had been.

It would happen just as God had warned, but few paid any heed. So Ezekiel preached and prophesied until one day God gave him a vision of a valley full of dry bones.

"Son of man, can these bones live?" asked God.

Ezekiel replied, "O Sovereign Lord, you alone know."

"Prophecy to these bones," God told him, "and say to them, 'Dry bones, hear the word of the Lord.'"

When Ezekiel had prophesied to the bones and the breath of God's Spirit had entered the bodies they came to life, and there before his eyes stood a vast army.

"These bones are the whole house of Israel," God explained. "I will make them one nation in the land on the mountains of Israel. There will be one king over all of them and they will never again be two nations or be divided into two kingdoms. . . .

My servant David will be king over them, and they will all have one shepherd. . . . And David my servant will be their prince for ever."

Although Ezekiel was not given any specific word of prophecy regarding the actual coming of the Saviour, God's Anointed One, his most significant prediction regarded the restoration of Judah and Israel to their own land as one united nation under God and under His chosen King.

The king, of course, would not be David himself, but the One from David's royal line who would be the Prince of Peace foretold by Isaiah. The prophets frequently spoke of David according to Hebrew usage, as being the King who would descend from David, and who would be Israel's final and everlasting King.

The son born to the virgin would be called Everlasting Father, Prince of Peace, and there would be no end to his rule. He would reign on David's throne because he would establish it in righteousness and justice forever, but that would be future. When the virgin's son came of age he would first be rejected as king, but he would later come to reign as their everlasting king.

"I will make a covenant of peace with them," said God. "It will be an everlasting covenant."

What a beautiful comforting picture of God's love and mercy! Cleansing, restoration, peace. No more unfaithfulness, wickedness and destruction. The Saviour would be the King, accepted not rejected, loved not hated, worshipped not reviled.

It was a picture of the far distant horizon, but it would come to pass because the Sovereign Lord had spoken.

Chapter 17

---※---

Where most of the prophets issued dire warnings to the people of Judah, Zechariah's prophecy was much more hopeful. He brought promise of a renewed and restored people returning, not only to their own land but also to their God.

The images which appeared to Zechariah in his visions were positive signs. The man with the measuring line indicated Jerusalem being measured in order to be rebuilt. Clean garments for the priests were symbolic of restored worship in the Temple, and the gold lampstand with the two olive trees meant that Israel would be restored, would be filled with the Spirit of God and would represent God's presence on earth.

"Shout and be glad O Daughter of Zion. For I am coming and I will live among you" God said.

The Lord's presence among them would be their ultimate joy; first as the Saviour coming to live among them, then later as the everlasting King.

"Here is the man whose name is the Branch," God instructed Zechariah to say.

The introduction of "The Branch", already mentioned by Isaiah and Jeremiah, clearly indicated the Branch from David's royal line who would come as promised.

"Rejoice greatly, O Daughter of Zion! Shout, Daughter of Jerusalem! See, your King comes to you, righteous and having salvation, gentle and riding on a donkey, on a colt, the foal of a donkey."

This is a lovely expression of the One who would come to bring salvation, while at the same time predicting an actual event in the life of that One. But the prophecy went further than the event because he would be the King, not just of the Jews but of the whole earth.

"He will proclaim peace to the nations. His rule will extend from sea to sea and from the River to the ends of the earth."

In deeply moving words Zechariah describes how compassionately God will deal with His people Israel when He brings in His Kingdom on earth.

"And I will pour out on the inhabitants of Jerusalem a spirit of grace and supplication. They will look on me, the one they have pierced, and they will mourn for him as one mourns for an only child, and grieve bitterly for him as one grieves for a firstborn son."

How wonderful to know that Israel will one day recognize God's Son, the Saviour as their rightful Messiah and King!

"On that day a fountain will be opened to the house of David and the inhabitants of Jerusalem, to cleanse them from sin and impurity."

It is significant that Zechariah prophesies that not only the house of David will mourn.

"The land will mourn, each clan by itself, with their wives by themselves: the clan of the house of David and their wives, the clan of the house of Nathan and their wives."

The house of Nathan, the second son of David and Bathsheba, has an important role to play in the coming of the Saviour.

Zechariah makes reference to another significant event in the life of the Saviour.

"If someone asks him, 'What are these wounds on your body?' he will answer, 'The wounds I was given at the house of my friends.'"

And yet again he foretells, "Strike the shepherd and the sheep will be scattered."

Zechariah's prophecy, full of deep pathos, yet wonderfully comforting, reaches a majestic climax when he declares, "On that day his feet will stand on the Mount of Olives, east of Jerusalem." And "Then the Lord my God will come, and all the holy ones with him."

And the final triumphant word: "The Lord will be king over the whole earth. On that day there will be one Lord, and His name the only name."

Chapter 18

———— ❈ ————

*M*icah prophesied during the reigns of Jotham, Ahaz and Hezekiah, kings of Judah and descendants of David. The period of his prophetic ministry was at a time when the king of Assyria was threatening to invade Jerusalem. Hezekiah, who was a good king, encouraged the inhabitants of the city to be strong and courageous in the face of this threat.

"Do not be afraid or discouraged because of the king of Assyria and the vast army with him," he told them, "for there is a greater power with us than with him. With him is only the arm of flesh, but with us is the Lord our God to help us."

Those who rely on God for help find that He gives them help, and in Hezekiah's day Jerusalem was not taken.

But the most important prophecy which Micah was given concerned the place of birth of God's Anointed One. Graciously God identified the exact location, and since He had already foretold that His Anointed would descend from David, it is no surprise that he would be born in the town of David's birth.

"But you Bethlehem Ephratah, though you are small among the clans of Judah, out of you will come for me one who will be ruler over Israel, whose origins are from of old, from ancient times."

Micah not only tells us where Israel's ruler, the Messiah would be born, but gives the fullest indication yet that "he" would come from the realms of the eternal.

"[His] origins are from of old, from ancient times."

This concurs with Isaiah's prophecy where he lists the names by which the ruler will be called – Mighty God, Everlasting Father, Prince of Peace.

Although he would be born of a woman, he would not be the son of a man. The Son would be given to the virgin in a miraculous way from God, his origins would be from of old, like God's, which is why he would be given God's names because God is his Father.

The revelation that God gave through His prophets tells us all we need to know about His promised Saviour, but even with it all we find it incredibly mysterious and something we will never fully be able to fathom. We just need to remember who God is, the Everlasting Father for whom nothing is impossible. He is Almighty God, the Creator of the ends of the earth, and He always had a plan to save the people He made and who sinned against Him.

With God all things are possible, and He is a loving and merciful God. He has gone to great lengths and great cost to show us how much He loves us.

Chapter 19

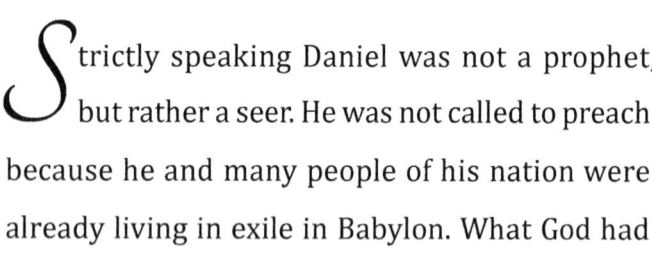

Strictly speaking Daniel was not a prophet, but rather a seer. He was not called to preach because he and many people of his nation were already living in exile in Babylon. What God had predicted earlier had already come to pass.

Daniel was given startling and awesome prophecies, far reaching in their scope, most of which related to the "end times". There was one striking exception. To Daniel was given a time scale for the coming of the Anointed One, the Messiah, the promised Saviour.

The angel Gabriel was sent by God to speak with Daniel. He had visited Daniel once before and had revealed to him a vision concerning the appointed time of the end, a vision which so appalled Daniel that he lay ill for several days.

Daniel was engaged in praying for his people and for the city of Jerusalem, confessing the sin of the nation to God, when Gabriel appeared to him a second time.

"Daniel, I have now come to give you insight and understanding," he told him.

As Daniel listened, Gabriel gave him the message sent from God.

" 'Seventy 'sevens' are decreed for your people and your holy city to finish transgression, to put an end to sin, to atone for wickedness, to bring in everlasting righteousness, to seal up vision and prophecy, and to anoint the most holy.'"

Biblical historians agree that the "seventy sevens" correspond to seventy periods of seven years which add up to 490 years, according to Hebrew usage. (ie they reckon a year as 360 days).

The angel Gabriel continued with further explanation.

"Know and understand this: From the issuing of the decree to restore and rebuild Jerusalem until the Anointed One, the ruler, comes, there will be seven 'sevens', and sixty-two 'sevens'. It will be rebuilt with streets and a trench, but in times of trouble. After the sixty-two 'sevens', the Anointed One will be cut off and have nothing."

The angel's message foretold that a decree would be issued to rebuild Jerusalem. No doubt Daniel and the other exiles could scarcely have imagined this happening, but Daniel believed the angel and recorded this encouraging prophecy.

Such a word of prophecy had also been given to Isaiah, years before, so it was already in God's plan before He sent the angel Gabriel to Daniel.

"I will raise up Cyrus in my righteousness ... he will rebuild my city and set my exiles free."

The decree was issued in the reign of Artaxerxes of Persia, and in c 445BC Nehemiah, an exiled Jew who served the king, asked and received permission to go to Jerusalem and begin rebuilding the city. History has confirmed that this took place as foretold.

Returning to the angel's message to Daniel, the "seventy sevens" are divided into three periods.

The first seven 'sevens' (49 years) refer to the time spent restoring Jerusalem from the date the decree was issued.

By adding on the second period of sixty-two 'sevens' (434 years) to the 49 years, this amounts to 483 years which is the time frame given for the appearance of the Anointed One.

According to Hebrew usage, (remembering that a year was 360 days), 483 years dating from 445BC brings us to 30AD, so this was the predicted time "to finish transgression, to put an end to sin, to atone for wickedness." This ties in perfectly with the Saviour's coming and purpose.

At the end of the 69 weeks,(seven 'sevens' and sixty-two 'sevens) when the Saviour had come He would be "cut off and have nothing." This we now know refers to his rejection by his own people. At that time the period of "everlasting righteousness" would not come in. It would still be future.

The angel Gabriel imparted further information to Daniel which would take place after the Anointed One left the scene: "The people of the ruler who will come will destroy the city and the sanctuary." Historically we know that Jerusalem and the Temple were destroyed by the Romans in AD70. The temple has never been rebuilt.

This leaves the 'seventieth' week to be fulfilled, and prophetically that period is still in the future. Daniel was given further information regarding it in other visions which deeply troubled him, and the angel told him, "Close up and seal the words of the scroll until the time of the end."

Importantly, the prophecy "to finish transgression, to put an end to sin, to atone for wickedness" was fulfilled. God kept His promise.

Chapter 20

———— ⁕ ————

*L*ong long ago in a garden the promise had been made. It was a tiny seed of a promise then, and it lay dormant in the depths of the dry soil for long ages.

Time went by, and at last the tiny seed began to sprout. Little by little it grew until a bud began to appear, and it would only be a matter of time until the bud would burst open into a beautiful blossom.

The Creator had sown this special seed in the garden, and He chose the prophets as His trustworthy gardeners to nurture the little seed until a full-blown plant would appear. He guided them and instructed them in its care until a strong plant was produced that was ready to be presented, not just to Israel but to the world.

In the beginning all anyone knew was that a Saviour had been promised, but as time progressed they learned more and more.

Gradually as the prophets shared their revelations over a period of time, the people of Israel discovered that a son would be born to a virgin, and he would be given wonderful heavenly names. He would be a descendant of King David, but would also have a divine origin. He would bring light and salvation and would minister to many. The time scale of his appearance was revealed and the specific location of his birth was identified. Now all they had to do was wait.

One other point was exceedingly important. By his coming all the nations of the world would be blessed!

Along with the prophecies concerning the Saviour, the prophets also warned Judah and Israel what would happen to them. They would be taken captive by the Assyrians, and a seventy year exile was allotted to them.

Then as God had promised they would be released from captivity and return to their own land. They would be united once more as the kingdom of Israel, but they would have only limited control of their land, and that only for a short time.

Before long other world powers would arise as Daniel had foretold, and look with envy on little Israel. First it was Greece, then Rome, and so it was that when the little seed of promise had matured and was ready to bloom, it found itself in a harsh and dangerous environment.

But it was all in God's plan and completely under His control. And so "when the time had fully come, God sent forth His Son, born of a woman."

Chapter 21

———— ※ ————

Her name was Mary. She was a direct descendant of Nathan, the second son of King David and Bathsheba! She was a young girl, not yet married, although betrothed to be married to Joseph, a member of her own clan of Judah. She lived in the little town of Nazareth in the region of Galilee up in Northern Israel.

It had startled and surprised Mary when an angel had appeared to her and greeted her in an extraordinary manner.

"Do not be afraid Mary," the angel told her. "You have found favour with God. You will be with child and give birth to a son, and you are to give him the name Jesus. He will be great and will be called the

Son of the Most High. The Lord God will give him the throne of his father David, and he will reign over the house of Jacob for ever; his kingdom will never end."

It was exactly as the prophets had foretold!

When she asked how this would come about the angel replied, "The Holy Spirit will come upon you, and the power of the Most High will over-shadow you. So the holy one to be born will be called the Son of God."

The Son of God! It would happen supernatu-rally! Through the power of the Holy Spirit! Mary did not question it, simply gave her response.

"I am the Lord's servant. May it be to me as you have said."

It must have been overwhelming for Mary, but she did not hesitate to commit herself to what God asked of her, although she knew it would not be easy.

The angel had told Mary that her cousin Elizabeth was going to have a child, so Mary hur-ried to Judea to see her. As soon as she entered the house the Spirit of God inspired Elizabeth to speak prophetically.

"Blessed are you among women, and blessed is the child you will bear! But why am I so favoured, that the mother of my Lord should come to me? As soon as the sound of your greeting reached my ears, the baby in my womb leaped for joy. Blessed is she who has believed that what the Lord has said to her will be accomplished!"

Her words must have been such a comfort to Mary, who, although so young, had been given such a daunting responsibility yet such a tremendous privilege by God. She too burst into praise, her words inspired by God's Spirit.

"My soul glorifies the Lord and my spirit rejoices in God my Saviour, for He has been mindful of the humble state of His servant. From now on all generations will call me blessed, for the Mighty One has done great things for me – holy is His name."

These two women recognized that the Saviour promised by God would soon be born and they were thrilled that each of them had a part to play in

His great plan. Elizabeth's son would be a prophet who would prepare the way for the Lord, and she acknowledged that Mary's son would be her Lord and Saviour. Mary too knew that the baby growing within her would not just be her son, but the Son of God, her Saviour too.

Mary finished her song of praise by referring to God's promise to Israel.

"He has helped His servant Israel, remembering to be merciful to Abraham and his descendants for ever, even as he said to our fathers."

Mary stayed until Elizabeth's son John was born, when his father Zechariah also prophesied by God's Spirit. Since he was a priest of the Levite clan and knew the scriptures well, he first spoke of Mary's son, even though he was not yet born.

"Praise be to the Lord, the God of Israel, because He has come and redeemed His people. He has raised up a horn of salvation for us in the house of His servant David (as He said through His holy prophets of long ago)."

Then Zechariah spoke concerning his own son.

"And you my child, will be called a prophet of the Most High; for you will go before the Lord to prepare the way for him, to give his people the knowledge of salvation through the forgiveness of their sins."

Mary must have been greatly blessed and encouraged as she returned home to Nazareth.

When Joseph learned that Mary was with child he was at first reluctant to marry her, but as he was pondering the matter an angel appeared to him too.

"Joseph, son of David, do not be afraid to take Mary home as your wife, because what is conceived in her is from the Holy Spirit. She will give birth to a son, and you are to give him the name Jesus, because he will save his people from their sins."

Was Joseph awed and thrilled by this revelation of the angel? He was a righteous man of God's chosen clan Judah and a direct descendant of King David through his son King Solomon. He would have known the Scriptures. Did he connect

Isaiah's prophecy regarding the virgin to Mary, his betrothed?

The angel had told him all he needed to know. The child Mary was carrying was "from the Holy Spirit". Rising from his sleep he did what the angel of the Lord had told him to do, and he brought Mary home as his wife. To him had been given the privilege and responsibility of protecting the precious Son of God and Mary his mother.

When Mary's baby was due to be born, the Roman Emperor Augustus decided to take a census of the entire Roman world which, at that time, included Israel. Everyone had to go to their own city to be registered, so since they were of the house and line of David this involved a journey to Bethlehem for Joseph and Mary. Bethlehem! Yes! The prophet Micah had foretold it!

"But you Bethlehem ... out of you will come for me one who will be ruler over Israel."

Bethlehem was David's city, and now God's appointed ruler from the clan of Judah would be born there. God had orchestrated world events to suit His plan so that His Anointed One, the Messiah, would be born in Bethlehem. He was in control, not Caesar Augustus.

Chapter 22

———— ❋ ————

*B*ethlehem was a busy place that night. Many weary members of the clan of Judah, obliged to come to the city because of the census, crowded into the little town, all seeking hospitality from their kinsfolk.

By the time Joseph and Mary arrived all the guest rooms had been filled, and they had to be content with a quiet corner of the quarters where the animals were housed. No doubt their relatives made it as comfortable as possible for them, but it was not a fitting place for a baby to be born, especially this baby! But God must have had His reasons. Perhaps the humble birth of His Son made him more accessible to ordinary folk. He did not come as a king, even though that would be his final destiny. He came as Son of the Promise.

Outside the town in the quiet dark fields, a group of shepherds were squatting on the ground chatting together while keeping an eye on their sheep.

Suddenly the darkness was shattered by the appearance of a heavenly being enveloped in glorious light. Terrified, the shepherds fell on their faces, scarcely daring to look up. The dazzling angel quickly reassured them.

"Do not be afraid. I bring you good news of great joy that will be for all the people. Today in the town of David a Saviour has been born to you; he is Christ the Lord. This will be a sign to you: You will find a baby wrapped in cloths and lying in a manger."

Momentous news! A Saviour! The shepherds could scarcely believe their ears, but before they could say a word they were surrounded by countless numbers of angels praising God in the most exquisite heavenly singing.

"Glory to God in the highest, and on earth peace to men on whom His favour rests."

The combination of sound and light was glorious. God had announced the arrival of His Son in a spectacular manner, a manner fitting for the tiny newborn king, who nevertheless had been born in such humble surroundings.

Once the angels had gone back up to heaven the thrilled and excited shepherds could scarcely contain themselves.

"Let's go to Bethlehem and see this thing that has happened, which the Lord has told us about."

That the Lord had made it known to them, simple shepherds, pleased and delighted them. So they hurried off to the town, and there they found it just as the angel had told them; a sweet little newborn baby, snugly swaddled and lying in a manger, with Mary hovering over him lovingly and Joseph smilingly looking on.

The shepherds, overcome with the sheer wonder of it all, told everyone they met about the newly-born long-awaited Saviour. As they returned to their sheep, still praising and glorifying God for everything they had seen and heard they were still talking excitedly about it all. It was the experience of a lifetime and it would stay with them forever!

Chapter 23

*T*he shepherds were not the only ones to rejoice at the birth of the Saviour.

Simeon, a dear old man of God, had been waiting with expectation for many years, and he enjoyed such a close relationship with the Almighty that the Holy Spirit revealed to him that he would not die until he had seen the Lord's Messiah.

One wonderful day the Holy Spirit led him to enter the Temple, and there he saw Mary and Joseph with the child Jesus whom they had brought to the Temple in Jerusalem to dedicate him to the Lord according to Hebrew custom.

Guided by God's Spirit, Simeon knew at once who this baby was. He reverently took him in his arms, and with deep emotion, gave thanks to God.

"Sovereign Lord, as you have promised, now dismiss your servant in peace. For my eyes have seen your salvation which you have prepared in the sight of all people, a light for revelation to the Gentiles, and for glory to your people Israel."

It was exactly as the prophets had foretold!

For Mary and Joseph it was an unexpected, but marvellous encounter. Simeon blessed them both, and then he spoke words to Mary which gave her much to meditate upon for many years to come.

"This child is destined to cause the falling and rising of many in Israel, and to be a sign that will be spoken against, so that the thoughts of many hearts will be revealed. And a sword will pierce your own soul too."

Prophetic words! What did they mean? The day when Mary would discover what they meant was still a long way off.

Just as Simeon finished speaking an old lady came up to see the baby. People, especially women, are always attracted by the sight of a tiny baby, and Jesus would have been six weeks old at this time, and at the stage where he was smiling and responding to people, as babies do.

This lady was the prophetess, Anna, who spent much of her time in the Temple, worshipping God, and as she smiled down at this little baby, she too gave thanks to God for the child Jesus, recognizing by God's Spirit that he was the promised Messiah.

Those such as Anna and Simeon, who devoted their lives to worship, prayer and study of the Scriptures, would have known from reading the Prophets that the time had drawn near for the fulfillment of God's promise to send the Saviour, and they were eagerly awaiting for it to happen.

That day in the Temple was a momentous day for them when God's Spirit revealed His precious Son to them. They were old, and they had waited long, but what joy, peace and contentment they experienced that day!

As for Mary and Joseph, they had much to think about and be thankful for as they left the Temple that day. They returned to Bethlehem, probably staying in the home of relatives in the town as it was the territory of clan Judah, and their kinsfolk would have extended hospitality to them as was traditional among them. It would have been a long way to travel with a young baby to their home in Nazareth, so for the time being they stayed put.

Chapter 24

———— ※ ————

A bright star shone in the sky, an unusually lustrous star, a new star, one they had never seen before. It had appeared suddenly, and the Magi gazed at it with great interest. They discussed it, speculated about it and gazed at it some more.

"What does it mean?" they wondered.

They consulted their scrolls, they talked and they meditated. Finally they reached a conclusion. The star indicated the birth of a new king!

The star continued to shine brightly. It was the greatest, most interesting phenomenon they had ever seen, and they had spent a lifetime studying the stars. It was intriguing, compelling. They just had to go and see the new king this star represented. He must be incredibly important!

So these eastern Magi who were also "kings" of small kingdoms, set out on the long journey to Jerusalem. They had figured out, probably because of the location of the star, that the king must be a king of the Jews, or perhaps God had revealed it to them for they were wise men who believed in Almighty God. The beauty and wonder of His creation, especially the skies, had fascinated them for a long time.

King Herod in his palace in Jerusalem was deeply disturbed by the arrival of these eastern kings.

"Where is he who has been born king of the Jews?" they asked, "for we have seen his star in the east and have come to worship him."

It was natural for them to assume that the new king would be born in Jerusalem, and clearly they did not know that Herod guarded his position as king exceedingly jealously. He had been granted his title and position by his Roman overlords, and he would brook no rival. Nevertheless, he knew enough about the Jewish religion to know that there was a prophecy of some kind regarding a Messiah who would arise for Israel, so he sent for the chief priests and teachers of the Law to find out where this king would be born.

The priests read from the book of Micah.

"In Bethlehem of Judea", they replied, "for this is what the prophet has written: 'But you Bethlehem, in the land of Judah, are by no means least among the rulers of Judah; for out of you will come a ruler who will be the shepherd of my people Israel'"

Herod spoke secretly with the eastern kings, craftily questioning them to find out when they had first seen the star. Then he told them to go and find the child.

"As soon as you find him, report to me, so that I too may go and worship him," he finished.

Unaware of Herod's cunning plan to find out the whereabouts of the new king, the Magi took their leave of him and journeyed towards Bethlehem. To their great delight they saw the same star which they had seen in the east shining brightly in front of them, and it led them directly to the house where Joseph and Mary and the baby were staying.

It was with awe and wonder that they knelt before him. They had a deep sense that this was he of whom the prophets had written, and they worshipped him, knowing that the little baby lying before them was the Anointed One who had been sent by God.

They had gifts for him because it was customary to bring presents to a king. Their offerings were also given in the sense of religious offerings to God as they worshipped this child: gold, frankincense and myrrh. The gold represented his kingship, frankincense was an aromatic herb used in sacrificial offerings, and was a token of his divinity, and the myrrh was used in perfuming ointments which would become significant later in his life.

The prophet Isaiah had prophesied regarding these visitors from the east.

"Nations will come to your light, and kings to the brightness of your dawn."

Words written hundreds of years before had come to fulfillment in these kings who had travelled all the way from eastern lands to see "the king of the Jews", God's Messiah.

As the Magi lay down to rest that night they were warned by God in a dream that they should not go back to Herod, so they returned to their own country by a different route.

They were no sooner gone than Joseph too had a dream in which God warned him to take the baby and his mother and flee to Egypt because Herod would seek to kill the young child.

Joseph arose immediately and left in the dead of night with Mary and the infant Jesus. They escaped to Egypt before Herod's soldiers arrived. The baby was safe. Later, when Herod had died, God instructed Joseph to return to his home in Galilee, and there it was that Jesus grew up, fulfilling the words of the prophet that "He shall be called a Nazarene".

Chapter 25

———— ✳ ————

*H*e was the first-born son of his mother Mary. Learning the trade of carpentry from his earthly father Joseph, he helped him in his carpenter's shop in the unpretentious little town of Nazareth in Galilee.

Then it was time. He was a young man of thirty years old when he knew the day had come to go out among his countrymen and women, and fulfill the purpose for which he had come into the world.

Jesus first went to the Jordan River where his cousin John was preaching and baptizing.

"I baptize you with water for repentance," John told the crowds who flocked to hear him, drawn from around the whole region , even from the city of Jerusalem.

"But after me will come one who is more powerful than I, whose sandals I am not fit to carry. He will baptize you with the Holy Spirit and with fire."

John cut a strange figure as he stood on the banks of the Jordan, clad in a garment made of camel's hair held in place by a leather belt. He was a passionate preacher, calling people to repent of their sin, and many responded to that call.

John had known early in his life that he had a special mission, and willingly he dedicated himself to his destiny. At his birth his father had prophesied.

"You my child, will be called a prophet of the Most High; for you will go on before the Lord to prepare the way for him, to give his people the knowledge of salvation through the forgiveness of their sins."

It was just as Isaiah the prophet had foretold!

As people began to wonder if John might possibly be the promised Messiah, he immediately denied it.

"I am not the Messiah," he declared.

"Then who are you?" he was asked.

"I am the voice of one calling in the desert, 'Make straight the way for the Lord'," he replied.

Never did John imagine that the One of whom he had been speaking would come to him for baptism, yet one day, out of the blue, he found Jesus standing before him asking to be baptized.

Humbly John spoke. "I need to be baptized by you, and do you come to me?"

"Let it be so now," Jesus replied gently. "It is proper for us to do this to fulfill all righteousness."

What did he mean by this?

Well, Jesus chose to be baptized because he wanted to fulfill all the conditions of Jewish religious Law. Water signified cleansing, and in Mosaic Law the priest was required to wash before offering a sacrifice, so Jesus submitted to the symbolic cleansing which consecrated him for the offering he would make of the sacrifice of himself for the sins of the world.

John understood, and as they went into the water together he knew it was a defining moment. Just as Jesus was coming up out of the water, both Jesus and John experienced God's spectacular power.

Jesus saw heaven being opened above him, and he saw God's Spirit descending upon him as a dove and remaining upon him, as God, his Father spoke to him.

"You are my Son, whom I love; with you I am well pleased."

Only God Himself could have said these words! And He could have said them only to Jesus, His Son. It is significant that all three persons of the Godhead were present in this encounter; Father, Son and Holy Spirit.

The descent of the Spirit on Jesus set the divine seal on his public ministry, and marked his coming as Messiah and the introduction of the kingdom of righteousness.

In the strength of this beautiful encounter he had with his Father, Jesus left to face a great testing in the desert before he began his earthly ministry.

John too, saw the Spirit descending upon Jesus. It enabled him to declare to the people the real identity of Jesus.

He had already spoken to the crowd in the preceding days about Jesus.

"Among you stands one you do not know," he had said.

Now he was able to tell them who this one was.

"I saw the Spirit come down from heaven as a dove and remain on him. I would not have known him, except that the One who had sent me to baptize with water told me, 'The man on whom you see the Spirit come down and remain is he who will baptize with the Holy Spirit.' I have seen and I testify that this is the Son of God."

This last statement was crucial. John had declared that Jesus was the Son of God, and he had it from the highest authority!

Chapter 26

$\mathcal{A}$fter Jesus had endured forty days of fasting and temptation in the desert, he returned first of all, for a few days to the Jordan where John was still preaching. He had faced Satan's onslaught in the power of God's Spirit and had been victorious. Now he was ready to begin his ministry in Galilee, just as the prophet Isaiah had foretold.

John saw Jesus coming towards him and drew the crowd's attention to him.

"Look, the Lamb of God, who takes away the sin of the world!"

John was fulfilling his mission. He was a prophet himself, and he was familiar with the writings of the prophets of old.

He continued, "This is the one I meant when I said, 'A man who comes after me has surpassed me because he was before me.' I myself did not know him, but the reason I came baptizing with water was that he might be revealed to Israel."

This was always John's intention, to draw all eyes away from himself and focus them on Jesus. His purpose was to reveal Jesus to the people of Israel.

The following day John spoke the same words again when he saw Jesus in the crowd.

"Look, the Lamb of God!"

John's mission had been to prepare the way for the Lord. He had preached repentance and had pointed to God's Son, so Jesus knew he would find among John's listeners people who would be willing to follow him. He had come back to the Jordan to choose some men who would become his disciples and accompany him as he travelled throughout the country.

John had a young disciple called Andrew. He was a fisherman from the town of Bethsaida in Galilee, and John's words struck a chord in Andrew's heart: "The Son of God, The Lamb of God!"

Andrew and his mate decided to follow Jesus. They spent the day with him, and by the time the day was done they knew they wanted to stay with him. Jesus too knew that he had found some friends.

The impact Jesus had upon Andrew and his friend was so powerful that Andrew could scarcely wait to tell his brother Simon.

"We have found the Messiah!" he told him excitedly.

Andrew brought Simon with him to meet Jesus, and when Jesus saw him he renamed him Peter, which meant "a stone" because he knew he had a special task for him later on in his life when the name would have significance.

Jesus only stayed a couple of days at the Jordan, and then he left for Galilee. It was to be the main centre of his ministry. Isaiah had said, "Galilee of the Gentiles, the people who walked in darkness have seen a great light." The darkness of the region of Galilee was about to be enlightened by "the light of the world".

Arriving in Galilee Jesus found a man called Phillip and said to him, "Follow me."

Philip immediately went to his friend Nathanael and told him, "We have found the one Moses wrote about in the Law, and about whom the prophets also wrote – Jesus of Nazareth."

"Nazareth! Can anything good come from there?" Nathanael exclaimed scathingly.

Undaunted, Philip simply said, "Come and see."

As he saw Nathanael approaching him, Jesus said, "Here is a true Israelite in whom there is nothing false."

"How do you know me?" Nathanael asked in surprise.

"I saw you while you were still under the fig tree before Philip called you," Jesus told him.

Now Nathaniel was impressed! Only the One of whom the prophets had written could know all about a person before he even met him.

"Rabbi, you are the Son of God, you are the King of Israel," he declared with conviction.

Chapter 27

————— ✳ —————

*A*s Jesus began teaching, preaching and healing throughout the region, people flocked to hear him and were amazed and excited about his teaching and the miraculous healings he performed, so his fame began to spread widely.

One Sabbath he returned to Nazareth, the town where he had grown up, and as he stood up to read in the synagogue, the scroll of Isaiah the prophet was handed to him. Isaiah had written many prophecies concerning him, and Jesus turned to one of them.

"The Spirit of the Lord is upon me because He has anointed me to preach good news to the poor. He has sent me to proclaim freedom for the prisoners and recovery of sight for the blind, to release the oppressed, to proclaim the year of the Lord's favour."

As all eyes were riveted on him he continued.

"Today this Scripture is fulfilled in your hearing."

Initially among the worshippers that day there was a sense of awe and expectation, but as they began to consider how someone they knew so well could be the One of whom Isaiah spoke, incredulity and disbelief crept in and they began to question his authenticity.

"Where did this man get these things?" they asked.

Others queried, "What is this wisdom that he has been given, that he even does miracles?"

They knew him as the son of Mary, who worked with Joseph in his carpenter's shop. They knew his brothers and sisters. How could this man who was one of themselves possibly be the one of whom Isaiah wrote? He was just an ordinary-looking man, nothing unusual about him, no sign to show that he was different from anyone else.

In spite of the miracles and gracious teaching they did not see him as being anyone exceptional. He was the boy next door, a carpenter, he had never studied to become a rabbi, so what right had he to be speaking about such spiritual matters?

Jesus, resigned to their disbelief, remarked, "Only in his home town, among his relatives and in his own house is a prophet without honour."

In the end they actually became furious with him and drove him out of the town with the intention of pushing him over the cliff on which the town was built. Emotions had run high because he was in effect saying that a prophet had no honour among his own because of their disbelief, and they were deeply offended.

Even so, it is still incredible that his own townsfolk would try to kill him. But although the religious leaders would finally succeed in doing just that, this was not the appointed time, and Jesus simply walked through the crowd and went his way.

It was his first rejection, and that it came from the people of his own town must have deeply saddened him.

The prophecies of Isaiah were already coming to pass in the life of the Saviour: "He was despised and rejected by men."

Chapter 28

*C*ompassion characterized his ministry. The sick, the disabled, the hungry, the poor, the marginalized were the recipients of his gracious attention.

As he travelled around the countryside he preached, he healed, he taught, he offered life abundant and life eternal, he drew people into the Kingdom.

His preaching placed great emphasis on the Kingdom. He was their Messiah, but he wanted them to understand that his Kingdom was not of this world.

Multitudes followed him, knowing he had something to give them that no-one else could give.

When he saw the crowds milling around him and looked at them with compassion, he saw them as sheep without a shepherd. They needed someone to look after them, teach them the truth about God, and give them hope.

The twelve men he had gathered about him as companions in his ministry needed to be trained, so he took them up to a mountain top and sat down with them. Crowds followed and soon there were many sitting at his feet drinking in every word he spoke.

As the sun shone on the grassy hillside, and a gentle mountain breeze fanned them, his blessed words dropped into the stillness while his audience sat as though spellbound. They knew within themselves that these words were truth and life.

"Blessed are the poor in spirit," he began, "for theirs is the kingdom of heaven."

Weren't they all poor in spirit, longing to know the grace of God in their lives? They kept their Mosaic Laws, made more burdensome than they were ever meant to be by their religious teachers, but did they know the peace, the joy, the contentment that truly knowing God would give them? Theirs was the kingdom of heaven, this young rabbi said.

"Blessed are those who mourn, for they will be comforted."

Many mourned, both from grief and from a sense of their own sin and unworthiness. How sweet to know that they would be comforted!

Those who hungered and thirsted after righteousness would be filled. How hungry they were! The food that this man offered them was nourishment for their hungry souls. What a blessing to be filled with spiritual food that would satisfy the deep need in their hearts!

The meek, the merciful, the pure in heart, the peacemakers, all would "see" God, see Him in such a way as to know Him and experience His blessing in their lives.

It was a different way of life from the dull ritualism and harsh legalism of keeping the Law, when everything was done for outward show, but inwardly their souls were dry and empty, though they ritually cleansed and paid their dues. They would be richly blessed in striving to be meek and merciful towards others, and in endeavouring to be peacemakers. Pureness of heart meant putting God first and keeping the heart free from impure thoughts and bitter feelings towards others.

"You are the salt of the earth," Jesus told them.

Salt adds flavour so they were to live life in such a way as to give something extra to the community in which they lived, so that people would see in their lifestyle something that was attractive and wholesome.

"You are the light of the world." Jesus said.

They were to make sure their light "shone" so that people would see that they were living as followers of their Lord, and that would result in glory to God.

"Do not think I have come to abolish the Law or the Prophets," Jesus continued. "I have not come to abolish them but to fulfill them."

He was Jewish. He kept the Law, but he put a new and fresh perspective on it. He himself was the fulfillment of the Law, but few, if any, recognized that fact just yet.

Take the commandment, "Do not kill" for example. Jesus extended that law to include being angry with friend, family or neighbour. There was to be no hatred in their hearts. They were not to allow their anger with anyone to reach the point where they were ready to harm them.

Before they could sincerely bring their offering to God in the Temple they must first be reconciled to the one with whom they were angry. They needed to come before God in the right spirit. It was not to be mere ritual, like the way the teachers of the Law practiced. Their worship to God should come from a pure and repentant heart.

"You have heard that it was said, 'Love your neighbour and hate your enemy' But I tell you: Love your enemies and pray for those who persecute you."

Radical teaching indeed!

Just as they were not to be angry with family or neighbour, neither was there to be malice towards their enemies. If their hearts were right before God, they were to put away any thoughts of hate and revenge towards anyone, either friend or foe. God sends rain and sunshine on both the evil and the good.

"Be perfect, therefore, as your Heavenly Father is perfect."

That was it in a nutshell. He was kind to all. And if He could show mercy and compassion, human beings were to follow His example.

"When you give to the needy, do not let your left hand know what your right hand is doing."

In other words their giving was to be done secretly, without letting other people know about it. Only God needed to know, and He would bless the giver.

Likewise prayer, an important part of Jewish life, was to be between the one who prayed and his or her God, to be done quietly in one's own home, and not where they could be seen to be praying, like the way the Pharisees prayed, "to be seen of men".

"Do not be like them," said Jesus, "for your Father knows what you need before you ask."

Then he gave them the beautiful hallowed prayer which has been prayed ever since, in every generation, each word significant in itself, recognizing God for the mighty and holy Being that He is, yet willing for us to call Him Father.

"Our Father in heaven, hallowed be your name,

Your kingdom come, your will be done on earth as it is in heaven.

Give us today our daily bread.

Forgive us our trespasses as we forgive those who trespass against us.

And lead us not into temptation, but deliver us from the evil one.

For yours is the kingdom, the power and the glory forever. Amen."

Jesus gave this prayer as a model of how we should pray; revering God's name, seeking His will, dependent on Him for our needs both physical and spiritual, needing His forgiveness, and recognizing His kingdom which is eternal.

Jesus emphasized the importance of forgiving others before we could expect forgiveness from

God, because holding an unforgiving spirit against others will destroy our peace, but with forgiveness comes peace; our peace with God, and the ability to live free from grudges against others, even when they hurt or distress us.

"Do not store up for yourselves treasures on earth," Jesus continued. Instead, "Store up for yourselves treasures in heaven."

It was much more important to fill their lives with doing good and keeping their thoughts on heaven, rather than spending all their energy on making money and having treasures in their homes which, after all, were subject to theft or decay.

"Do not worry about your life, what you will eat or drink; or about your body, what you will wear. Is not life more important than food, and the body more important than clothes?"

In beautiful poetic language worthy of the Lord and Creator of the Universe, Jesus, Son of God explained why we should not worry.

"Look at the birds of the air; they do not reap or store away in barns, and yet your heavenly Father feeds them. Are you not much more valuable than they? Who of you by worrying can add a single hour to his life?"

So simple! God feeds the birds, so there is no doubt that He will feed us as well. And He does!

Long ago He gave this promise:

"As long as the earth endures, seedtime and harvest, cold and heat, summer and winter, day and night will never cease."

"And why do you worry about clothes?" Jesus asked. "See how the lilies of the field grow. They do not labour or spin. Yet I tell you that not even Solomon in all his splendour was dressed like one of these. . . . . Will He not much more clothe you, O you of little faith?"

One more exhortation he gave them before leaving the subject. They could be sure that God would feed and clothe them, but one other important thing was needed.

"Seek first His kingdom and His righteousness, and all these things will be given to you as well."

Before he left the mountain he taught them not to be judgemental.

"Do not judge, or you too will be judged. For in the same way as you judge others, you will be judged.... Why do you look at the speck of sawdust in your brother's eye and pay no attention to the plank in your own eye?"

In plain language, if we judge others we can expect to be judged ourselves. Jesus pointed out that it is foolish to blame other people for minor offences when we might well be guilty of much greater wrongs. That is being hypocritical, and he was harder on the hypocrites than on anybody.

"Ask and it will be given to you; seek and you will find; knock and the door will be opened to you. For everyone who asks receives; he who seeks finds; and to him who knocks, the door will be opened."

How encouraging this was to his hearers! They could ask God for His forgiveness and His help in their lives, if they looked for Him they would find Him, and if they knocked at His door He would open it and let them in. He is a God who loves to communicate with all of His creation, and He is reachable and approachable when we "ask, seek, and knock" in prayer.

Jesus had talked at length, his hearers listening avidly, but at last he came to a final summing up of his teaching thus far.

"So in everything, do to others what you would have them do to you, for this sums up the Law and the Prophets."

What a different place the world would be if everyone heeded that precept!

There were narrow roads and broad roads, symbolically speaking, he told them. The gate was wide and the road broad that led to destruction and many entered through this gate. It was a much easier gate to find and a much easier road to travel but it would lead to destruction.

"Enter through the narrow gate," he urged them.

It was a small gate and a narrow road but it would lead to life. Sadly only a few would find it, but it could be found if one searched for it. He longed that they would seek and find it.

Jesus concluded his great "sermon on the mount" with another illustration, painting a vivid picture of the wise as opposed to the foolish person.

The wise were those who listened to his words and put them into practice. They were like a man who built his house on a rock. The rain came down, the streams arose, the winds beat and blew against that house, yet it did not fall because it had its foundation on a rock.

On the other hand there was the foolish man who did not heed his words. He built his house on the sand, and when the rain came down, the winds battered against the house and the streams arose the house fell down with a great crash.

His audience got the picture! And they were amazed at his teaching because he taught as one who had authority, and not as their teachers of the Law.

Chapter 29

———— ✳ ————

*J*esus placed great emphasis on the Kingdom of God. He longed that people would seek to enter it, and there was only one way.

One evening he had a visit from a Pharisee. This was unusual because generally the Pharisees did not approve of him and were constantly criticizing him.

Nicodemus seemed to be interested though. Something about Jesus had caught his attention and he wanted to know more.

"Rabbi, we know you are a teacher who has come from God," he began. "For no-one could perform the miraculous signs you are doing if God were not with him."

Was it a statement or a question? Did Nicodemus really believe that Rabbi Jesus had come from God? It is certain he realized that no-one could do such miracles without God's power, but he was hovering on the edge of belief and disbelief. Was Jesus really who he claimed to be? Nicodemus wanted to know.

"No-one can see the kingdom of God unless he is born again."

Jesus' response completely confused Nicodemus. How on earth could one be born again?

So Jesus explained.

"No-one can enter the kingdom of God unless he is born of water and the Spirit. Flesh gives birth to flesh, but the Spirit gives birth to spirit."

It was a spiritual matter, nothing to do with natural birth, but Nicodemus didn't quite get it.

"How can this be?" he asked.

Jesus expressed surprise that a religious teacher would not understand these things, but he explained further. Firstly he confirmed the opening observation Nicodemus made that he was a teacher who had come from God.

"No-one has ever gone into heaven except the one who came from heaven – the Son of Man."

Jesus often referred to himself as Son of Man because of his human ancestry.

Then he went on to say, "Just as Moses lifted up the serpent in the desert, so the Son of Man must be lifted up, that everyone who believes in him may have eternal life."

Nicodemus, being a teacher of the Scriptures, was familiar with the incident in the desert. It dated back to the time when Moses was leading the Israelites out of Egypt, and they were complaining so bitterly against Moses and against God that God allowed them to be bitten by poisonous snakes and many died.

This brought them to their senses and they came to Moses and said, "We sinned when we spoke against the Lord and against you. Pray that the Lord will take the snakes away from us."

So Moses prayed, and God told him, "Make a serpent and put it up on a pole; anyone who is bitten can look at it and live."

God always provided a remedy for sin.

Moses told the Israelites to look and live, and Jesus was now telling Nicodemus to do the same: look at the Saviour and live. The raised pole was symbolic of Jesus himself, and later on Nicodemus would fully understand exactly what Jesus meant.

Meantime Jesus spoke the amazing words which have become the best-known verse in the Bible, a verse which everyone from a Christian background, and even many without this background, have known since childhood.

"For God so loved the world, that He gave His only Son, that whoever believes in him shall not perish but have eternal life."

It is the most supreme expression of love the world has ever known. God loved and He gave – His greatest gift to the world, the Saviour.

In the beginning the man and the woman sinned and lost their innocence and their immortality, but God always had a plan to restore mankind, so He sent His Son as He promised. If men and women believed in him and accepted him they would have the eternal life that had been lost in the "fall". God would give it back to them, though at great cost to Himself.

"God did not send His Son into the world to condemn the world, but to save the world through him," Jesus told Nicodemus.

Jesus did not come into the world to condemn people. That is not what a Saviour does. The Saviour came to save. He came to draw sinners into his kingdom with his love. He came to give his life as the sacrificial lamb: as John said, "The Lamb of God who takes away the sin of the world."

Nicodemus left that night with much to think about.

Chapter 30

The Pharisees were a force to be reckoned with. When they were not pulling Jesus up on some minor point in the Law, they were questioning him about everything he said, criticizing everything he did, accusing him of being in league with the devil, and all the time plotting how they could get rid of him.

Often they thought they had an ironclad case against him, but Jesus was more than a match for them, and they always came off as the losers in any encounter.

One morning when he was in the Temple courts with the people all gathered around him, he sat down and began to teach them. It wasn't long before the Pharisees and teachers of the Law appeared, and this time they had brought with them a woman who had committed adultery, which of course was against the Law.

Almost rubbing their hands with glee as they were sure they would trap him, they began their questioning.

"Teacher, this woman was caught in the act of adultery," they began.

(Really? In the act? Where was the man?)

"In the Law Moses commanded us to stone such women. Now what do you say?"

Jesus did not say anything at first. He simply bent down and began to write on the ground with his finger. He finally straightened up and spoke as they continued to bombard him with questions.

He looked them straight in the eyes and said, "If any one of you is without sin, let him be the first to throw a stone at her."

They were beaten. They could not withstand the power of his reasoning, and self-righteous though they were, they knew they were not without sin themselves. One after another they left.

Jesus looked at the woman standing before him and asked, "Woman, where are they? Has no-one condemned you?"

"No-one, sir," she replied.

"Then neither do I condemn you," said Jesus. "Go now and leave your life of sin."

In this case Jesus could see the injustice against this woman, and knew the Pharisees had only brought her to him to try and trap him. According to their reasoning, if he said she should not be stoned he would be breaking the Law, but if he said she should, then he would be showing a complete lack of justice and mercy. There would be no justice for her if she was the only one convicted since clearly someone else was involved as well.

So Jesus did what he always did – got to the heart of the matter. He challenged the Pharisees about their own sin and showed them to be hypocrites, and he also faced the woman with her sin.

In this personal encounter with Jesus the poor, frightened, guilty woman saw love and mercy as she looked into the eyes of the Son of God. He did not condemn her because, as he had told Nicodemus, he did not come to condemn but to save. He forgave her, and taught her to leave her life of sin.

She went away forgiven and un-condemned, owing her very life and eternal soul to the one who had shown her mercy and forgiveness.

Jesus was harder on hypocrites than on anyone else, and the Pharisees were surely hypocrites. He pointed out how they loved the best seats in the synagogues, they dressed to look as "religious" as possible, prayed long prayers in public to be seen and heard, disfigured their faces to look as though they were fasting, gave their alms where everyone could see, and generally did everything outwardly so that they would appear like godly religious observers of the Law.

But they would have shown no mercy to the woman who committed adultery. With them there was no forgiveness for sinners, but there was with Jesus.

"I did not come to call the righteous, but sinners to repentance," he declared.

Only Jesus had the power to forgive sins as he demonstrated when he told a paralytic man, "Friend, your sins are forgiven."

The Pharisees at once protested, saying, "Who is this fellow who speaks blasphemy? Who can forgive sins but God alone?"

"Why are you thinking these things in your hearts?" asked Jesus. "Which is easier: to say, 'Your sins are forgiven,' or to say, 'Get up and walk'? But so that you may know that the Son of Man has authority on earth to forgive sins," he then said to the paralytic, "Get up, take your mat and go home."

Everyone praised God saying, "We have seen remarkable things today."

Chapter 31

———— ✵ ————

*J*esus was asked on one occasion, "Which is the greatest commandment?"

"Love the Lord your God with all your heart and with all your soul and with all your mind, and with all your strength," Jesus said. "This is the first and greatest commandment. And the second is like it: 'Love your neighbour as yourself.' There is no commandment greater than these."

This summarized perfectly the Ten Commandments given by God to Moses. God's purpose in giving these laws was to ensure that people lived safe, happy and fulfilled lives. If they loved and revered God in the way He set out in the first four commandments, they would have a good relationship with Him. And if they loved others as set out in the remaining six laws they would all live in a safe and peaceful community. Murder, stealing, adultery, disrespect for parents, false witness and covetousness brought devastation in their wake.

There were numerous other rules and regulations contained in the Judaic Law to which the Pharisees and religious leaders strictly adhered. They focused greatly on the rituals of the Law. They were interested in the outward, visible demonstration of the Law. They prayed, they fasted, they gave their tithes, but they did it outwardly.

"To be seen of men," Jesus said.

There was a better way. Love and honour God, and love and respect your fellow man.

The religious leaders accused Jesus of keeping the wrong company, sinners and the like; he neglected ritual cleansing, he broke the Sabbath, he didn't encourage his disciples to fast. They saw him as a law-breaker.

Jesus was justified in calling them hypocrites. What use was outward ritual cleansing if inwardly their hearts were full of unkind thoughts towards others? Why fast, pray and tithe just to be seen? Good in themselves, they needed to be carried out in the right spirit; an attitude of worship towards God.

Jesus said to them, "Whoever hears my word and believes Him who sent me has eternal life and will not be condemned."

They professed to worship God but they took offence at Jesus calling God his Father, so in their eyes he was not only a Law-breaker, but in claiming God as his Father he was making himself equal with God. This they could not tolerate.

Jesus provided them with specific evidence that God was his Father.

"You have sent to John and he has testified to the truth," he told them.

They had chosen, for a time at least, to believe John because he had descended from the Levitical priesthood and so had a good religious pedigree which carried great weight with them. He had spoken of Jesus and declared him to be the Son of God.

But Jesus had further evidence. His miracles attested that God the Father had sent him. No-one could do the things he had done without the power of God.

"And the Father who sent me has Himself testified concerning me," Jesus said. "You have never heard His voice not seen His form, nor does His word dwell in you, for you do not believe in the one He sent."

Then there was the Scriptures which, as religious teachers, they knew very well.

"You diligently study the Scriptures because you think by them you possess eternal life," Jesus told them.

Yes, the Scriptures were important to them, very important. But there was so much they missed!

"These are the Scriptures that testify about me," Jesus said.

There was no denying it. The Prophets had foretold him in so many different ways: when he would come, where he would come, where he would come from, why he would come, how he would minister – to the sick, the poor, the broken-hearted.

"Yet," said Jesus sadly, "You refuse to come to me to have life. I have come in my Father's name and you do not accept me."

One final piece of evidence Jesus gave them before leaving the subject. This was powerful evidence because they focused so strongly on Moses.

"If you believed Moses, you would believe me, for he wrote about me."

This was a strong challenge to them. Moses had recorded what God had told him to say.

"I will raise up for them a prophet like you from among their brothers. I will put my words in his mouth, and he will tell them everything I command them."

Jesus pointed out their foolishness to them. They were all talk. They professed to hold Moses and the Law in the highest possible esteem. Yet did they really believe what Moses said?

"Since you do not believe what he wrote, how are you going to believe what I say?"

Did they take seriously what Moses said about him, or did they overlook its importance in their obsession of keeping the letter of the Law?

"You refuse to come to me to have life."

It must have broken his heart to say it. He loved them, all of them, Pharisees, everybody. He had come to them to give them life, but they would not come to him.

"I am the light of the world," he told them. "Whoever follows me will never walk in darkness, but will have the light of life."

"In him was life, and that life was the light of men," his disciple John later declared.

He taught the crowds, healed many, fed them physically and spiritually, but he loved to reach out to individuals in their need, whatever that need might be. His love was so great, his mercy and com-passion so boundless, that when he met a needy person he touched their life in such a way that they would never be the same again.

Chapter 32

So it was with the widow in the town of Nain where Jesus and his disciples had gone with the usual large crowd in his wake. Just as they entered the town they met a funeral procession. Many mourners accompanied the widow who was burying her only son.

Jesus' heart went out to her and he went over to her, saying gently, "Do not weep."

At that he turned around and placed his hand on the coffin. Then in his power, authority and compassion he spoke.

"Young man, I say to you, get up."

At once the young man arose and with great joy his mother received him back again from the hands of Jesus. While the mother and son were joyfully reunited the crowd was filled with awe. They had just witnessed an amazing miracle.

"A great prophet has appeared among us," they said. "God has come to help His people."

Zacchaeus, the tax-collector was another recipient of Jesus' loving concern. This time Jesus was in Jericho where Zacchaeus lived. Being a collector of taxes involved working for the Roman Government, therefore he came in for scorn and even abuse from the citizens of Israel who hated having to hand over a hefty proportion of their hard-earned cash to their hated overlords.

Zacchaeus was a chief collector, and wealthy, but with it came loneliness and isolation.

He heard about Jesus and he was filled with a great need and desire to see him. He rushed out of his house and ran to where the crowd was surrounding Jesus, but he was so short that he couldn't catch a glimpse of the Lord at all, so he ran ahead and climbed a tree so that when Jesus passed by he could get a good look at him.

What expectations did this lonely, wealthy little man have? He wanted to see who Jesus was, and something within him longed to hear the things that Jesus was saying, but he probably had no idea that Jesus would touch his life in a powerful way. Imagine his surprise when Jesus stopped at the foot of the tree.

"Zacchaeus, come down. I would like to come to your house today."

Amazed and delighted, Zacchaeus at once climbed down and welcomed Jesus gladly to his home.

The crowd was not well pleased. Mumbling and grumbling they said, "He has gone to be the guest of a sinner."

Tax collectors were regarded as sinners because they hob-nobbed with the enemy. But they were human beings with hearts to be comforted and souls to be saved just like anyone else, and it was to such as these that Jesus came to minister.

Zacchaeus was a changed man after his encounter with Jesus. He had experienced compassion and acceptance from Jesus, and that had been so lacking in his life. He felt he wanted to reciprocate in some way.

"Lord," he announced, "Here and now I give half of my possessions to the poor, and if I have cheated anyone of anything, I will pay back four times the amount."

A generous offer indeed! He would give away a great deal of his riches. They no longer seemed so important to him because he had found something much more precious.

Jesus commended him and pointed out a few home truths to the people listening.

"Today salvation has come to this house, because this man too, is a son of Abraham. For the Son of Man came to seek and to save what was lost."

We must not write people off, Jesus taught, just because they were living life in a way of which we disapprove. No-one can see into another's heart, only Jesus could do that, but he encouraged people to look with compassion on everyone. They all needed salvation, and he had come to save them.

"He who believes has everlasting life."

Chapter 33

— ✳ —

*J*esus had many personal encounters with people because he could see right into the heart of every individual, and he longed to meet their need.

Once on his way back to Galilee Jesus decided to go through Samaria because he knew there was someone in that town who needed to meet with him.

She was standing by Jacob's Well in the mid-day heat when Jesus approached her and asked her for a drink of water.

"You are a Jew and I am a Samaritan woman. How can you ask me for a drink?" she queried.

Jews and Samaritans were not really on speaking terms because of their past history. They despised each other and did everything they could to avoid each other. In addition men did not speak to women they did not know, yet here was Jesus breaking down all the barriers.

His heart went out to this woman, and he came right to the point.

"If you knew the gift of God and who it is who asks you for a drink, you would have asked him and he would have given you living water."

Mystified, the woman gazed at him for a moment before she found her voice.

"Sir, you have nothing to draw with and the well is deep. Where can you get this living water?"

She must have looked at him wonderingly, a strange thought dawning in her mind.

"Are you greater than our father Jacob, who gave us the well, and drank from it himself?"

Jesus' answer went straight to the heart of the matter.

"Everyone who drinks this water will be thirsty again, but whoever drinks the water I give him will never thirst. Indeed the water I give him will become in him a spring of water welling up to eternal life."

Eternal life! What kind of water could this be? Jesus' words resonated deeply with this despised and lonely woman with the thirsty soul.

"Sir, give me this water so that I won't get thirsty and have to keep coming here to draw water."

Sooner or later an encounter with Jesus always brought people face to face with their sin.

"Go, call your husband and come back," Jesus said to her.

The woman admitted she didn't have a husband.

"You are right when you say you have no husband." Jesus told her calmly. "The fact is, you have had five husbands, and the man you now have is not your husband. What you have just said is quite true."

The woman, who by now must have been greatly intrigued by the behavior of this Jewish man, realized he was different from anyone she had ever met.

"Sir, I can see you are a prophet," she began. Then seeking to better understand, she continued, "Our fathers worshipped in this mountain, but you Jews claim that the place where we must worship is Jerusalem."

Jesus answered her implied question, and told her that the time had come for all true worshippers to worship the Father in spirit and in truth; Jews, Samaritans, Gentiles, it made no difference, worshipping God the Father was a spiritual matter.

"God is Spirit," Jesus declared, "and His worshippers must worship in spirit and in truth."

In response the woman said, "I know that Messiah is coming. When he comes he will explain everything to us."

Then, standing there in the afternoon heat, the simple words, spoken by Messiah himself, dropped into the stillness.

"I who speak to you am he."

She must have gazed at him in wonder and speechless joy before the return of the disciples dispelled the special moment.

The woman was so excited, and so eager to share her wonderful news, that she left her water pot lying by the well, and hurried back to the town.

"Come, see a man who told me everything I ever did. Could this be the Messiah?"

Oh, she knew he was the Messiah all right! Perhaps she just wanted to give others the chance to discover this for themselves.

They came, running from the town to the place where Jesus was still waiting. He knew they would come. The needy woman whose life he had touched, was a changed woman, and she had shared her new-found life, hope and joy with everyone, so they wanted to find out who or what had changed her.

When they met him they understood. They were captivated by his words, and they begged him to stay with them and tell them more.

During the two days he was able to remain with them, many many more came to faith as they too believed he was the Messiah.

Initially they had believed because of the woman's testimony. Now they had met him and heard for themselves.

"We know that this man really is the Saviour of the world," they declared.

Chapter 34

When the Pharisees and religious teachers taught in the synagogues it was as dull as ditchwater, all about the "do's" and "don't's" of the Law, but when Jesus taught, his teaching was about the kingdom of heaven, and he brought it to life with short pithy little parables and fascinating stories which illustrated perfectly the important points he wanted to make.

Crowds followed him everywhere, eager to hear everything he had to say because they could see that he taught with authority, and not like the Pharisees.

When he climbed a sunny hillside to get away for a short while by himself, it was not long before they found him, so he sat down and taught them.

When he went to sit by the lake hoping to have a few minutes rest and quiet, they crowded around him, so he stepped into a boat at the water's edge and spoke from there to the crowds on the shore.

Jesus grew up among the people of Galilee so he knew all about the lifestyles of farmers, fishermen, shepherds, and housewives, so accordingly he used scenes and situations they were familiar with to illustrate the truths he wanted them to understand.

The stories of a shepherd going out to the rough terrain of the hills in search of a lost sheep, the woman who searched her house for a lost coin, the father watching and waiting every day for his wayward son to some home, were touching illustrations of how God longs for and waits for and seeks his lost children.

When the shepherd found his lost sheep he brought it home on his shoulder rejoicing.

When the woman lost one of her precious silver coins, she lit a lamp and swept the dark corners of her house until she found it.

The lost son had wandered far from home and dabbled in all sorts of dodgy practices, but when he finally came to his senses and returned home his father was waiting for him with open arms and welcomed him warmly.

"In the same way," said Jesus, "there is rejoicing in the presence of the angels of God over one sinner who repents."

The stories demonstrated that it was always worthwhile seeking the lost, and that there was always rejoicing when the lost were found.

Men and women are lost without God and have been since the fall in the Garden of Eden, but God was not content to leave it there. His plan was always to send Jesus, the Saviour.

"I have come to seek and to save those who are lost," said Jesus.

He wanted to find them and return them to the place where they would get to know God and have a loving relationship with their Creator, just as Adam and Eve had done before they sinned.

"No-one comes to the Father except through me," said Jesus. "I am the way."

He was the way into the kingdom of God, and there was no other way.

When the Pharisees asked when the kingdom of God would come, Jesus replied, "The kingdom of God does not come with your careful observation, nor will people say, 'Here it is,' or 'There it is,' because the kingdom of God is within you."

It was a spiritual matter. People entered the kingdom by believing and repenting, and he told another little parable to make this clear to the Pharisees who were asking these questions.

"What do you think?" Jesus questioned them. "There was a man who had two sons. He went to the first and said 'Son, go and work today in the vineyard.'"

The son said he wouldn't go, but later he changed his mind and went. Meanwhile the man asked his second son to go and he agreed, but then didn't bother going.

"Which of the two did what his father wanted?" asked Jesus.

"The first," they answered without hesitation.

Exactly! They were right!

"The tax collectors and the prostitutes are entering the kingdom ahead of you," said Jesus. "For John came to show you the way of righteousness, and you did not believe him, but the tax collectors and the prostitutes did. And even after you saw this you did not repent and believe him."

Chapter 35

—— ※ ——

*A*s time went on Jesus began to be even more specific in his teaching on the kingdom of God, especially to the religious leaders.

"Listen to another parable," he said.

This was a sad and sombre tale of a landowner who owned a vineyard. He did everything possible to protect it, building a wall around it, setting up a watchtower, and placing the wine press within its precincts.

He rented the vineyard out to some farmers and went away on a journey. When harvest time came around he sent his servants to collect his fruit, but the tenant farmers treated the servants despicably, stoning and killing them until there were no more left to send.

Finally the landowner sent his son.

"They will respect my son," he said.

But when the tenants saw him coming they said, "This is the heir. Come, let us kill him and take his inheritance."

"When the owner of the vineyard comes, what will he do to these tenants?" Jesus asked.

Not yet realizing that Jesus was making a point about their attitude in this story, they answered readily.

"He will bring these wretches to a wretched end," they replied, "and he will rent the vineyard to other tenants, who will give him his share of the crop at harvest time."

"'The stone the builders rejected has become the capstone'" Jesus quoted from the Scriptures. "Therefore I tell you that the kingdom of God will be taken away from you and given to a people who will produce its fruit."

They realized then that Jesus was talking about them. They had refused to believe in him, and had openly opposed him, and Jesus knew they wanted to kill him.

When they sent temple guards to arrest Jesus and they came back without him, they asked, "Why did you not bring him in?"

"No-one ever spoke the way this man does," the guards declared.

Sadly the leaders were not willing to enter the kingdom, and they, along with all who refused to believe in him, would lose their opportunity because of their unbelief and outright rejection.

The parable of the wedding banquet had a similar theme.

"The kingdom of heaven is like a king who prepared a wedding banquet for his son," Jesus told them. "He sent his servants to those who had been invited to the banquet to tell them to come, but they refused to come."

They all made excuses, this that and the other, and they too seized his servants, ill-treated them, and even killed them.

So this king sent other servants out into the highways and byways to bring in whoever they could find, for the banquet was prepared and ready. Soon the banqueting hall was filled and the king was pleased.

In this story the king represented God, the son represented Jesus, and the wedding feast was symbolic of the time at the end of the world when Jesus would bring his bride, the Church, home to heaven. The Church would be made up of all who believed in him from every nation in every generation.

The story was not quite finished however, so Jesus added another important observation.

At the wedding banquet there was one man who was not wearing wedding clothes.

"Friend, how did you get in here without wearing wedding clothes?" the king asked.

Jesus was making an important point in this parable. The wedding clothes are symbolic of "the robe of righteousness" with which we must be clothed before we can enter heaven. It just simply means that when we believe, repent and have our sins forgiven we are figuratively "clothed with his righteousness" and therefore fit to enter into God's presence.

The parable of the weeds was another little allegory which Jesus used to describe the kingdom of God.

"The kingdom of heaven is like a man who sowed good seed in his field. But while everyone was sleeping, his enemy came and sowed weeds among the wheat, and went away. When the wheat sprouted and formed ears, then the weeds also appeared."

As Jesus continued the story he explained that the enemy of the kingdom was Satan, so the weeds, which were his, would grow along with the wheat, which was God's, until harvest time. The harvest represents the end of the world, and when that time comes there will be a distinction between those who belong to God's kingdom and those who do not.

Those who rejected God's Son would not be part of the kingdom. It was a sombre thought. But for those who accepted Jesus, God's Son, there would be great joy.

"They will shine like the sun in the kingdom of their Father," said Jesus.

There were numerous other little stories Jesus used to illustrate the kingdom. As usual he used events and objects from their everyday lives.

"The kingdom of heaven is like a mustard seed," he told them.

From the tiniest of seeds would sprout a tree large enough to provide shelter for the birds.

It was like yeast which a woman mixed into the flour and it expanded until the dough trebled in size and was baked into a substantial loaf of bread.

It was like treasure hidden in a field, a pearl of great value, a net let down into the lake which caught all kinds of fish. The man who found the treasure sold all he had to buy it because he had found something of great value. Likewise the merchant who found the pearl sold everything he had to obtain it. The net full of fish was pulled up on the shore, and the bad fish discarded but the good ones retained.

"This is how it will be at the end of the age," said Jesus. "The angels will come and separate the wicked from the righteous."

It was a solemn warning. Jesus really wanted them to understand. The kingdom of God was precious, like a gem, and those who entered it would inherit eternal life. But there was the other side of the coin. Those outside the kingdom would face separation from the bliss of God's presence in His everlasting Kingdom.

Chapter 36

---

*J*esus performed numerous miracles, but the gospel writer John, who was one of his twelve disciples, and therefore an eye-witness, records seven as being significant because they demonstrate that Jesus, as Creator, could change the laws of nature at will. Nothing was impossible to him. His miracles are proof that he came from God.

John, of all the gospel writers, is the one who makes sure from the very first, that we understand that Jesus "was with God in the beginning" and that "through him all things were made." He reinforces Micah's prophecy that his "origins are from of old", making it clear that he was co-eternal with God.

When Jesus changed the water into wine at the wedding feast which he attended in Cana, he did so by an act of his will. He did not touch the water which became wine. He simply told the servants to fill the water pots with water and then serve it to the guests. The point is that Jesus had power over the created order to change it. He created the water in the first place, so he could just as easily change its substance.

This was the first miraculous "sign" which John recorded. The second sign which he mentions is the healing of the nobleman's son. This man, a royal official, said to Jesus, "Sir come down before my child dies," to which Jesus replied, "You may go. Your son will live." Again, Jesus' word was enough to accomplish this miracle.

John's third "sign" involved the healing of a man at the Pool of Bethesda in Jerusalem. Jesus performed many miracles of healing while he was in Jerusalem during one of the religious feasts, but this one was unusual because rather than someone coming to him to ask for healing, Jesus initiated the conversation.

"Do you want to get well?" he asked this man who had been crippled for thirty-eight years.

"Sir, I have no-one to help me."

He had no-one for thirty-eight years, but now he had Jesus!

"Get up! Pick up your mat and walk," said Jesus simply.

Immediately he was cured, so he did what Jesus told him, even though it was the Sabbath, which of course brought down the wrath of the Pharisees upon Jesus.

The fourth "sign" was the feeding of five thousand men plus women and children. That was a lot of people sitting on a hillside in late afternoon, hungry, but so enthralled by everything Jesus was telling them that they did not leave to go home and eat.

Taking the five small loaves and two little fish which a little boy had given him, Jesus first of all gave thanks for them, and then, as he broke each piece of bread and fish it became a miracle in his hands, in this way superseding the laws of nature as he fed the multitude, all of whom had enough and more as there were lots of fragments left.

Like the water into wine, six large stone pots of it, which tasted better than anything the guests had drunk earlier, Jesus always gives in abundance.

The people who were so miraculously fed declared, "Surely this is the Prophet who is to come into the world."

Jesus made the first of his "I am" statements after this miracle. He offered spiritual food which would forever satisfy them.

"I am the bread of life," he told them. "He who comes to me will never go hungry, and he who believes in me will never be thirsty."

On another occasion when he was teaching, Jesus said, "I am the light of the world."

He wanted them to know that whoever followed him would have 'the light of life' because his light shines in the darkness of this world. It was the second of his "I am" statements.

The fifth "sign" was a spectacular feat which had the disciples at first frightened and then awed. It was late in the evening and they were crossing the lake in their boat when the water suddenly became rough and the wind stormy. They were rowing frantically when they spotted through the gloom, a figure walking on the water, and they were terrified because they thought it was a ghost.

Jesus quickly reassured them, "It is I. Don't be afraid."

So they took him into the boat, and immediately the sea was calm.

This mighty miracle, which again superseded the laws of nature, caused the disciples to declare, "Truly you are the Son of God."

Chapter 37

$\mathcal{T}$he healing of the man born blind, which John records as the sixth "miraculous sign", had the Pharisees hopping mad! They did everything they possibly could to have Jesus discredited and condemned, constantly questioning the man, and repeatedly passing judgment on Jesus.

Like so many of Jesus' miracles it took place on the Sabbath which upset the deeply religious Pharisees. Jesus had previously pointed out that it was right to do good on the Sabbath, but they would have none of it. They themselves would have rescued their donkey if it had fallen into a pit on the Sabbath, but to heal a person who had been ill for years on the Sabbath was totally out of the question! That was work! So it couldn't be done on the Sabbath.

This healing was different from other healings for several reasons. In the first place the man was blind from birth, secondly he did not ask for healing, and thirdly Jesus used a different method of healing. He made some mud with soil and saliva and put it on the man's eyes.

Then he said, "Go and wash in the Pool of Siloam."

When this man, who had always been blind, returned from washing in the pool, people began to question whether he was the same blind man who had sat begging in the street.

Some claimed he was the same man, others said that he only looked like him, but the man himself said, "I am the man."

There was no sign of Jesus by now, so the man told the bystanders what Jesus had done, but didn't know where he was or anything else about him.

Then the Pharisees became involved. People brought the man to them, because they were, after all, the religious experts, so they wanted to know what the Pharisees thought of this healing.

Their first comment was, "This man is not from God for he does not keep the Sabbath."

Never mind that the man who had never been able to see since birth could now see!

But the miracle couldn't be ignored, so some asked, "How can a sinner do such miraculous signs?"

"What have you to say about him?" the man was asked. "It was your eyes he opened."

"He is a prophet," replied the man.

The religious leaders couldn't quite believe that this man had ever been blind and now had sight, so they sent for his parents.

"Is this your son?" they asked. "Is this the one you say was born blind? How is it that he can now see?"

The parents confirmed that he was their son, but declined to make any comment on how he could now see because they feared that they would be put out of the synagogue.

"Ask him," they said. "He is of age; he will speak for himself."

So back they went to the man who could now see.

"Give glory to God," they said. "We know this man is a sinner."

"Whether he is a sinner or not, I don't know," said the man. "One thing I do know. I was blind but now I see."

Once again they asked him, "How did he open your eyes?"

"I have told you already and you did not listen. Why do you want to hear it again? Do you want to become his disciples, too?"

"You are this fellow's disciple!" they shouted angrily, hurling insults at him. "We are disciples of Moses! We know that God spoke to Moses, but as for this fellow, we don't even know where he comes from."

"Now that is remarkable!" the man retorted. "You don't know where he comes from, yet he opened my eyes."

Then he really angered these self-righteous hypocritical teachers of the Law with some very discerning remarks.

"We know that God does not listen to sinners. He listens to the godly man who does His will. Nobody has ever heard of opening the eyes of a man born blind. If this man were not from God he could do nothing."

This made them livid with rage.

"You were steeped in sin at birth; how dare you lecture us!"

The contrast between these self-righteous, know-all religious teachers, and an ordinary man, who up till now couldn't see and had sat begging in the streets, is remarkable. It is fair to say that their fundamentalism went too far. The letter of the Law, according to the Pharisees, had to be kept, and those who didn't keep it were condemned.

That they rejected the healer of this man and condemned his as a sinner was outrageous. And it was grossly unfair to treat the now-seeing man with such contempt. They actually threw him out of the synagogue.

When Jesus met with him later on, as usual he came straight to the point.

"Do you believe in the Son of Man?" he asked.

"Who is he, sir?" the man asked. "Tell me so that I may believe in him."

Like the Samaritan woman, here was a thirsty soul genuinely seeking to know the truth.

Again in this personal encounter with this man, Jesus spoke the wondrous words he had spoken before to the Samaritan woman.

"You have now seen him; in fact he is the one speaking with you."

"Lord, I believe," the man said instantly, and he worshipped Jesus. He had been healed both physically and spiritually. He could see with his eyes, and also with his heart, and he acknowledged Jesus as his Healer and his Saviour.

Chapter 38

———— ✳ ————

"*I* am the good shepherd. The good shepherd lays down his life for the sheep."

This was the third of the "I am" statements that Jesus made about himself.

The image of a shepherd with his sheep was an appropriate one for the Messiah. He had sometimes been described by the prophets as the Shepherd of Israel.

When talking to the crowds around him, many of them now believing followers, it was how he saw himself and how he saw them. When he had first sat on the grassy slopes to teach them, he saw them as sheep without a shepherd with no-one to care for them, give them pasture, lead them beside quiet waters, like his human ancestor David who had been a shepherd before he became a king. Jesus too was both shepherd and king, and he wanted to shepherd his flock.

It was a pleasing illustration. Sheep grazed among the hills throughout the country, and the sight of a shepherd leading his sheep in and out of the sheep pen to feed in the meadows was a familiar pastoral scene. There was something comforting and reassuring about it.

So Jesus talked to them about his role as a shepherd. He knew each of his sheep by name, he told them. Each was precious to him, so he warned them to watch out for the stranger who was not a shepherd, who only wanted to harm them like the stranger in the Garden of Eden. If his own sheep followed him they would know his voice, and they would not go astray. He would lead them out to find pasture, and he would bring them safely back into the sheep pen to rest at night.

But he cared deeply for those who were not yet in his fold.

"I have other sheep that are not of this sheep pen. I must bring them also," he said.

Like the shepherd in the little parable he had told, he would go out to seek the lost sheep and when he found it he would bring it home with rejoicing. He so much longed to bring everyone into his kingdom.

"I lay down my life – only to take it up again. No-one takes it from me, but I lay it down of my own accord. I have authority to lay it down and authority to take it up again. This command I received from my Father."

It was God's plan. Jesus would willingly give up his life, but that would not be the end. When he had fulfilled his mission he would return to his Father.

The prophet Isaiah wrote, "We all, like sheep, have gone astray, each of us has turned to his own way; and the Lord has laid on him the iniquity of us all."

Jesus took the analogy of the sheep and shepherd a little further when he told those listening,

"I am the gate; whoever enters through me will be saved."

It was his fourth "I am" statement. He was telling the people that he was not only the shepherd who would lead them into the sheep pen, but he was the actual gate into the sheepfold.

"The thief," he said, "comes only to steal and kill and destroy; I have come that they may have life, and have it to the full."

He warned again about the evil one, who wanted to keep them out of the safety of the sheep pen. He would rather destroy them like a wolf attacking a sheep, but Jesus, the shepherd would give them life in all its fullness.

He is the gate into the sheep pen, and he is the shepherd who cares for the sheep.

"I know my sheep and my sheep know me."

Chapter 39

*J*ohn's seventh and final "sign" which he recorded in his gospel, involved three special friends of Jesus. They were three siblings who lived in Bethany, not far from Jerusalem. Jesus loved them very much and visited them as often as he could.

Martha was probably the eldest, quite bossy, a woman of action, and the organizer of the family. Her sister Mary was gentler and more contemplative, and her brother Lazarus could possibly have been called "the quiet man" because in the several stories told of them, no word of his is recorded.

Martha loved to entertain, and whenever Jesus came to call she bustled about preparing food and setting it on the table with great delight. But while Martha concocted delicious food in the kitchen, Mary just liked to sit and listen to Jesus.

Once, everything got too much for Martha. Jesus called, along with his disciples, to her home where Martha set about preparing a meal for them all. But with so many people present she found it impossible to do it all by herself, so, distracted, she went to Jesus.

"Lord, don't you care that my sister has left me to do the work by myself?" she demanded. "Tell her to help me!"

"Martha, Martha," the Lord said to her with gentle rebuke. "You are worried and upset about many things, but only one thing is needed. Mary has chosen what is better, and it will not be taken away from her."

It would seem from subsequent events that Martha took to heart what Jesus said, and like Mary, she too spent some time listening to Jesus, learning from him and coming to realize exactly who he really was.

The day came when their brother became ill, very ill, and the sisters sent word to Jesus.

"Lord, the one you love is sick."

Because they knew Jesus loved them they expected him to come right away and heal Lazarus.

However, when he got the word, Jesus said to his disciples, "This sickness will not end in death. No, it is for God's glory so that God's Son may be glorified through it."

He stayed on where he was two more days, then he decided to go back to Judea.

The disciples at once remonstrated with him.

"But Rabbi," they said, "a short while ago the Jews tried to stone you, and yet you are going back there?"

"Our friend Lazarus has fallen asleep; but I am going there to wake him up," he told them.

They thought he meant Lazarus was resting in sleep, but Jesus told them plainly that Lazarus was dead.

"For your sake I am glad I was not there, so that you may believe," he added.

So the disciples decided to accompany him even though it might mean death for them as well.

By the time Jesus and the disciples reached Bethany, Lazarus had lain in the tomb for four days and the sisters were heartbroken. Many of their neighbours and friends came to comfort them, but they longed for Jesus.

As soon as Martha heard he was coming, she, being a lady of action, hurried off to meet him while Mary stayed in the house. Without preamble, she spoke her mind as soon as she saw Jesus.

"Lord, if you had been here, my brother would not have died. But I know that even now God will give you whatever you ask."

"Your brother will rise again," Jesus said to her.

"I know he will rise again in the resurrection at the last day."

Then Jesus spoke those immortal words that are the essence of the assurance within all of us who believe that we will rise to eternal life.

Was the world standing still to hear as he declared this sublime truth?

"I am the resurrection and the life. He who believes in me will live, even though he dies; and whoever lives and believes in me will never die."

It was his fifth "I am" statement. Martha, to whom these blessed words were first spoken, must have found them deeply moving in the midst of her sorrow.

"Do you believe this?" Jesus asked.

"Yes, Lord," Martha replied unhesitatingly. "I believe that you are the Messiah, the Son of God who was to come into the world."

What a special moment this was for Martha and for the disciples who were standing around!

With the renewed hope and comfort that her meeting with Jesus had given her, Martha returned to her house and called Mary aside.

"The Teacher is here and is asking for you," she whispered.

So Mary got up at once and accompanied Martha to the place just outside the village where Jesus had met her. All the neighbours, and there were many, saw her going out and followed her, thinking she was going to the tomb to mourn there.

Mary, who was accustomed to sit at Jesus' feet learning from him, now knelt before him.

"Lord, if you had been here my brother would not have died," she wept.

It distressed Jesus deeply to see the sorrow of his friends Mary and Martha. The many others who had gathered around were weeping too, and Jesus completely understood how they felt. Death was the result of the fall in the Garden of Eden. It was a sad fact of life, but he had come to defeat death.

"He who believes in me will live, even though he dies," he had said.

Death would be defeated in him because he was the resurrection and the life.

"Where have you laid him?" he asked.

"Come and see, Lord."

The grief of others grieved Jesus too, and he wept. They were face to face with the reality of death, and Jesus felt the pain of his friends as they led him to the tomb. His sadness was visible as the tears poured down his face.

"See how he loved him!" the people observed.

Some of those following him to the tomb said, "Could not he who opened the eyes of the blind man have kept this man from dying?"

Of course he could have kept Lazarus from dying, but if he had, it would not have brought such glory to God, or brought so many to faith, so ultimately he had a purpose in Lazarus' death.

Jesus, still deeply moved, approached the tomb which was a cave in the rocks with a stone laid across the entrance.

"Take away the stone," he instructed.

But practical, outspoken Martha deterred him.

"But, Lord," she said bluntly, "by this time there is a bad odour, for he has been there four days."

"Did I not tell you that if you believed, you would see the glory of God?" said Jesus quietly.

So Martha permitted them to move the stone.

As Jesus stood in front of the open tomb, he looked up towards heaven and prayed.

"Father, I thank you that you have heard me. I knew that you always hear me, but I said this for the benefit of the people standing here, that they may believe that you sent me."

When he had finished praying, he called in a loud voice, "Lazarus, come out!"

As everyone stood with bated breath, the astounding miracle took place, and a figure emerged bound hand and foot with strips of linen and with a cloth around his face.

"Take off the grave clothes and let him go," said Jesus.

As Lazarus was unbound Martha and Mary received him back joyfully, and the people standing around put their faith in Jesus who had wrought this awesome miracle. To bring back from the dead one who had already been in the grave for four days was something that they knew only the Son of God could do.

But for the many who believed, incredibly there were others who went away and told the Pharisees, and they were so alarmed that they called a meeting of the Sanhedrin. This council included the chief priests, scribes, Pharisees and Sadducees who were the chief religious leaders.

"What are we accomplishing?" they asked each other. "Here is this man performing many miraculous signs. If we let him go on like this, everyone will believe in him, and then the Romans will come and take away both our place and our nation."

Currently, the Romans allowed the Jews to practice their own religion in return for keeping the peace, and so far they had succeeded in doing so. The Sanhedrin feared that the people, who believed he was the Messiah, would want to make him king, and that could cause an uprising. If there was a rebellion the Romans would quickly quell it and take away the privileges they had given the chief religious leaders of the people. They professed that by dealing with Jesus themselves that would be the end of the matter, and there would be no further trouble.

Caiphas, the high priest even prophesied unknowingly, "It is better for you that one man die for the people than that the whole nation perish."

How could these religious leaders fail to believe that Jesus was the Messiah? There was so much evidence in the miracles he performed, especially this last one. A body in the grave for four days would be in a decaying state, and his soul would have departed to the abode of the believing dead. That such a person could be brought forth from the grave with his body and soul reunited could only be the work of God. It would be utterly impossible to anyone else.

Perhaps, in their heart of hearts they believed, but chose to put themselves first, so that they could maintain the status quo, and retain the special privileges they had under Rome.

Or perhaps their eyes were completely blinded, and they had no spiritual understanding whatsoever, despite being religious leaders – "the blind leading the blind" as Jesus once said.

Chapter 40

---※---

After the miraculous raising of Lazarus from the dead, when the religious leaders began plotting in earnest to arrest Jesus, he no longer moved around in public, so he spent his time privately with his disciples.

Then six days before the Passover he began to travel towards Jerusalem, stopping in Bethany again where a dinner was given in his honour. It took place in the house of a man called Simon, but Jesus' friends Martha, Mary and Lazarus were all in attendance.

As usual Martha served. That was the best way she knew how to demonstrate her love to the Lord.

Lazarus sat at the table with Jesus, quiet as usual, keeping his thoughts to himself.

Mary had chosen a unique way to express her love and gratitude. She opened an alabaster box of expensive perfume which she poured on Jesus' feet, and then wiped his feet with her hair. Mary's heart was full. Her sins which were many had all been forgiven, she had her beloved brother restored to her, and she loved the Lord at whose feet she had so often sat, listening and taking in every word of his wonderful teaching.

She showed her devotion with a costly gift, but she considered him worthy of such a gift. The whole house was filled with the fragrance of the perfume, and Jesus appreciated her token of love.

There were those who found fault though with Mary's action. Judas Iscariot, one of the disciples, complained of the extravagance and said the perfume should have been sold and the money given to the poor.

"Leave her alone," said Jesus. "She has done a beautiful thing to me. She poured perfume on my body beforehand to prepare for my burial. You will always have the poor among you, but you will not always have me."

Even here at this private dinner given for Jesus, many people found out that he was there, and they came, not only to see Jesus, but to see Lazarus as well. Clearly Lazarus was an interesting phenomenon and they wanted to see him and no doubt question him, but if he talked about his experience none of the gospel writers recorded it.

Bethany was only a couple of miles from Jerusalem, so on the day following the dinner, Jesus and his disciples began their journey towards the city.

Jesus had already warned his disciples several times that he was going to be put to death, but they seemed unable to comprehend it. Now on their way towards Jerusalem for the Passover Feast he told them plainly once again in order to prepare them.

"We are going up to Jerusalem, and the Son of Man will be betrayed to the chief priests and the teachers of the Law. They will condemn him to death and will turn him over to the Gentiles to be mocked and flogged and crucified. On the third day he will be raised to life."

Many of the prophecies written about Jesus had already come to pass, but those that still remained were about to be fulfilled.

Just before they entered the city Jesus sent two of his disciples on an errand.

"Go to the village ahead of you," he instructed, "and at once you will find a donkey tied there, with her colt by her. Untie them and bring them to me. If anyone says anything to you, tell him that the Lord needs them, and he will send them right away."

The colt was young and Jesus had ensured that the mother donkey came with her colt so that neither would be distressed. It was characteristic of his compassion for all that he had made. He, the Creator of all things cared about all of his creation.

He chose to ride on the little colt into Jerusalem. It fulfilled Zechariah's beautiful prophecy.

233

"Rejoice greatly O Daughter of Zion .. see, your king comes to you, gentle and riding on a donkey, on a colt, the foal of a donkey."

That Jesus was willing to enter Jerusalem riding on a donkey indicated that he was preparing for the events which would follow. He wanted the people to know that he was their Messiah, but equally he wanted them to know that he was their Saviour.

He was not entering the city as a conquering king with an army behind him to take over from the Romans. He was the Lamb of God, the sacrifice for all the people, even though he really was their king, but his kingdom was not of this world.

Jerusalem was full to capacity. Crowds from all across Israel came to the city for the annual Passover Feast, and in addition many from the Diaspora came too, and the place was packed.

The excited crowd who followed him that day waved palm branches and even laid their cloaks on the ground for him as he approached.

"Hosanna to the Son of David," they sang. "Blessed is he who comes in the name of the Lord. Blessed is the king of Israel!"

They knew the prophets had foretold that Messiah would be a son of David, and they were also quoting from Zechariah.

How completely accurate were the prophecies concerning him! It is interesting to note that Zechariah had made it clear that he was righteous, gentle and had salvation, meaning that he came as Saviour and not as king. Few, if any would have understood this at the time.

When Jesus reached Jerusalem, visitors to the city and others who had not yet encountered him asked, "Who is this?" and the many who already knew him informed them.

"This is Jesus, the prophet from Nazareth in Galilee."

With a few days left before the Passover Feast, Jesus continued to teach and heal mainly in the temple courts, but when the religious leaders saw what he was doing, and heard children shouting, "Hosanna to the Son of David!" they were furious.

"Do you hear what these children are saying?" they asked him.

"Yes," replied Jesus. "Have you never read, 'From the lips of children and infants you have ordained praise'?"

They still continued to harass him, asking, "By what authority are you doing these things? And who gave you this authority?"

"I will ask you one question," Jesus replied. "If you answer me I will tell you by what authority I am doing these things. John's baptism – where did it come from? Was it from heaven, or from men?"

As they discussed it, they knew if they said it came from heaven Jesus would ask why they did not believe it, and if they said it was of man they were afraid of the people who believed John to be a prophet, so they took the easy way out and said they did not know.

"Neither will I tell you by what authority I am doing these things," said Jesus.

Once again their attempt to score over Jesus ended in failure, and as they saw how the people were running after him and believing in him, they were becoming more and more anxious to find a way to be rid of him once and for all.

"See, this is getting us nowhere," they said. "Look how the whole world has gone after him!"

As it happened, a chance to arrest him came their way from a completely unexpected source. It would only be a matter of time and then they would have him!

Chapter 41

$\mathcal{D}$eeply saddened by the rejection of the religious leaders, and knowing that the time was drawing near for him to leave the world and return to his Father, Jesus withdrew from public ministry and spent his remaining hours with his disciples. There was little time left, and he wanted to use what there was to instruct and encourage them before he left them.

The time for the Passover Feast had arrived.

"Where do you want us to make preparations for you to eat the Passover?" the disciples asked Jesus.

"Go into the city, and a man carrying a jar of water will meet you," said Jesus. "Follow him. Say to the owner of the house he enters, 'The Teacher asks: Where is my guest room, where I may eat the Passover with my disciples?' He will show you a large upper room, furnished and ready. Make preparations for us there."

The disciples did as they were instructed, and when evening came Jesus arrived with his disciples and found the room prepared and ready. This Passover meal was the last supper he would eat with all twelve of them.

They were all reclining at the table when Jesus got up and did something very unusual. He took off his outer cloak, wrapped a towel around his waist, poured water into a basin, and began to wash his disciples' feet. The washing of feet was normally done by a servant, but Jesus wanted to show his disciples two things through this act: firstly how much he loved them, and secondly how they should love and care for each other.

When he came to Simon Peter the impetuous fisherman was not pleased.

"Lord, are you going to wash my feet?" he demurred, clearly disapproving.

"You do not realize now what I am doing, but later you will understand," Jesus told him.

"No, you shall never wash my feet," said Peter.

"Unless I wash you," said Jesus, "you have no part with me."

At that Peter submitted because, although he disapproved of Jesus, the Teacher, doing this menial task, he genuinely loved the Lord and wanted to be part of his ministry team.

After he had finished washing their feet Jesus returned to the table and explained to them the significance of what he had just done. He had set an example for them to follow.

"You call me 'Teacher' and 'Lord', and rightly so for that is what I am. Now that I, your Lord and Teacher have washed your feet, you also should wash one another's feet."

The mood among the disciples was already sombre after the feet washing, but now Jesus became even more solemn as he faced the twelve men who had accompanied him throughout his three year ministry.

"I have eagerly desired to eat this Passover with you before I suffer," he said to them. "For I tell you I will not eat it again until it finds fulfillment in the kingdom of God."

The disciples probably did not understand what Jesus meant, or why he wanted to share this Passover with them, and in particular why he wanted to give it a special meaning.

It would all become clear later, but Jesus knew he only had a few hours left to teach them and prepare them for all that would follow. There was deep symbolism in his words and actions, and later they would remember and understand.

Taking a cup of wine, Jesus gave thanks and said, "Take this and divide it among you. For I tell you, I will not drink again of the fruit of the vine until the kingdom of God comes."

There were four cups of wine associated with the Passover which were taken at specific points during the feast. This was possibly the second one because after it came the breaking of bread, which was unleavened bread, symbolic of the "eating in haste" when the Israelites were leaving Egypt.

Jesus took the bread, gave thanks, broke it and gave it to his disciples.

"This is my body given for you; do this in remembrance of me," he said.

After he broke and distributed the bread, Jesus lifted another cup of wine, possibly the third, and spoke words of deep significance and symbolism.

"This cup is the new covenant in my blood which is poured out for you."

We know these words of institution as Communion, Eucharist or the Lord's Supper.

After they had all drunk of this wine which initiated the "new" covenant, Jesus looked around sadly at those at the table with him.

"One of you is going to betray me," he said sorrowfully.

They were shocked and saddened. As they stared at each other around the table, one after another said, "Surely not I Lord!"

Peter motioned to John to ask Jesus who he meant.

"Lord, who is it?" John whispered.

"It is the one to whom I will give this piece of bread when I have dipped it in the dish."

Dipping the bread, Jesus handed it to Judas Iscariot.

"What you are about to do, do quickly," Jesus told him quietly.

As soon as Judas had taken the bread he left. Going out into the darkness of the night he went to commit his diabolical act of betrayal.

The other eleven men scarcely noticed him going. They were still questioning and arguing over other matters as they reclined at the supper. Only Jesus knew he had gone, and where and why he had gone.

"Now is the Son of Man glorified and God is glorified in him," he said.

As he looked around at the disciples Jesus continued to prepare them for his departure.

"My children, I will be with you only a little longer. You will look for me, and just as I told the Jews, so I tell you now: Where I am going you cannot come."

Then he continued to speak in the same theme with which the evening had begun. He wanted them to know the importance of love in their dealings with each other.

"A new command I give you: Love one another. As I have loved you, so you must love one another. By this all men will know that you are my disciples, if you love one another."

Chapter 42

―――― ✳ ――――

*A*s the hours passed on his last evening with them, Jesus spoke words of deep comfort, gave them wonderful promises, and encouraged them to keep on loving and serving him and each other.

"Do not let your hearts be troubled," he said. "Trust in God, trust also in me."

He had fully demonstrated that God was his Father, and he had been acknowledged by John, and by many who met him, heard him and saw his miracles that he was the Son of God. So, since he was the Son of God they could trust in him too.

"I am going [to my Father's house] to prepare a place for you. And if I go and prepare a place for you, I will come back and take you to be with me that you also may be where I am. You know the way to the place where I am going."

In spite of all they had seen and heard over the three years they had spent with Jesus did the disciples really understand?

Incredibly Thomas questioned, "Lord, we don't know where you are going, so how can we know the way?"

"I am the way," said Jesus simply. "I am the way, the truth and the life. No-one comes to the Father except through me."

It was beautifully simple. There is only one way to God, and that is through Jesus. "I am the way" – it was the sixth of his seven "I am" statements.

But there were still questions. They were still unclear.

"Lord, show us the Father," said Philip.

Patiently Jesus replied, "Don't you know me Philip, even after I have been with you such a long time? Anyone who has seen me has seen the Father. How can you say, 'Show us the Father'?"

He had already declared that God was his Father and had talked to them often about his relationship with God, his Father. How was it that they still didn't get it?

"Don't you believe that I am in the Father, and that the Father is in me? The words I say to you are not just my own. Rather, it is the Father living in me who is doing His work."

He had taught them so much over the three years he had spent with them, they had watched him turning water into wine, walking on the surface of the sea, raising the dead to life. Didn't they understand who he was? They themselves had declared him to be the Messiah, the Son of God. Didn't they believe it?

"Believe me when I say that I am in the Father and the Father is in me;" Jesus urged them. "Or at least believe on the evidence of the miracles themselves."

Then, in words of both challenge and encouragement, he let them know that they were to carry on his work, the ministry of preaching, teaching and healing.

"Anyone who has faith in me will do what I have been doing. He will do even greater things than these, because I am going to the Father."

What did he mean?

Firstly they could ask in prayer, and secondly they would have divine help.

"I will do whatever you ask in my name, so that the Son may bring glory to the Father. You may ask me for anything in my name, and I will do it."

They would not be asked to do anything in their own strength. Although Jesus was leaving them he assured them they would not be alone.

"I will ask the Father and He will give you another Counsellor to be with you for ever – the Spirit of truth."

This was an entirely new concept to them. Jesus explained further.

"The world cannot accept Him, because it neither sees Him nor knows Him. But you know Him, for He lives with you and will be in you. I will not leave you as orphans; I will come to you."

They were silent. At this moment in time they were unable to comprehend it all.

"Before long, the world will not see me any more, but you will see me," Jesus continued. "Because I live, you also will live. On that day you will realize that I am in my Father, and you are in me, and I am in you."

What did it mean to be "in" him and he "in" them?

When the time came for Jesus to leave the earth, and his physical presence was no longer with them, God would send the Counsellor to be with them. He would not only be with them, He would dwell within them because He was the Spirit of the Son, and the disciples would be secure in the knowledge that they were united to him as they believed and trusted in him.

"If anyone loves me, he will obey my teaching," he told them. "My Father will love him, and we will come to him and make our home with him."

God the Father and Jesus the Son loved them! It surely must have been comforting to them as it still is to us today.

"All this I have spoken while still with you," continued Jesus. "But the Counsellor, the Holy Spirit, whom the Father will send in my name, will teach you all things and will remind you of everything I have said to you."

They knew of the Holy Spirit, but they had not yet experienced Him. As these Jewish men listened to these amazing words, their own spirits must have been stirred within them. They could not comprehend it all, it was so new and different from anything else Jesus had yet said, but it would have filled them with awe and wonder.

Then, to calm their hearts, Jesus gave them a blessing.

"Peace I leave with you; my peace I give you. I do not give to you as the world gives. Do not let your hearts be troubled and do not be afraid."

Peace of mind and heart and soul. They need not be troubled, no matter what. His peace would be within them. It was like the time they were out in the boat in rough seas, but once Jesus entered the boat there was a great calm.

He had power to calm the troubled heart as well as the stormy sea.

"I will not speak with you much longer," Jesus told them, "for the prince of this world is coming. He has no hold on me."

Jesus knew time had run out for him. The prince of this world, meaning Satan, was "coming" in the guise of Judas and the religious rulers, to mount his final assault on Jesus while he was on the earth, but he would find no sin or weakness in Jesus that he could use against him. He would not win. He would be crushed.

"But the world must learn that I love the Father and that I do exactly what my Father has commanded me," Jesus said finally.

He was willing to go through with his Father's will, the plan God had from the beginning to send the Saviour who would atone for sin and "pour out his life unto death".

Chapter 43

———— ✳ ————

The meal over, Jesus said, "Come now, let us leave."

As they left the upper room to go out into the dark night, Jesus continued his teaching.

As at the beginning of his ministry when he turned water into wine to demonstrate the joy and bounty of the kingdom, he turned his thoughts again towards the vine to which he likened himself. And if he was the Vine, his followers were the branches.

"I am the true vine," he said. It was the seventh and final "I am" statement.

"I am the true vine, and my Father is the gardener. Remain in me, and I will remain in you. No branch can bear fruit by itself; it must remain in the vine. Neither can you bear fruit unless you remain in me."

This is really another little parable. The vine is comprised of the main stem and the branches, and just as the branches of a vine draw their strength and fruitfulness from the stem, so believers will draw their spiritual power from Jesus, the Vine.

Believers who maintain their closeness to the Lord, and understand that they can do nothing without him, will experience his strength and grace in their daily lives, and be enabled through him to live godly and useful lives as they share their faith and point others towards the Saviour. They cannot do it in their own strength. Only by dwelling in their Lord can they achieve the fruitfulness that he wants from them. Then the joy and abundance of his kingdom will be spread around.

"As the Father has loved me, so have I loved you. Now remain in my love," he said.

The love of the Saviour ran deep; just how deep they would witness very soon.

"If you obey my commands you will remain in my love. My command is this: Love each other as I have loved you."

Love is at the heart of it all. It is the most powerful force in the world, and Jesus' love was so deep that he was prepared to lay down his life for the world that he loved.

Jesus was able to say, "Greater love has no-one than this, that he lay down his life for his friends."

As they walked, Jesus continued to teach, instruct and encourage. Life would be tough for them, but there would be his grace, his peace, even his joy. He spoke again of the Counsellor. He, when He came, would remind them of everything Jesus had taught them, and guide them in the truth. Just now they were confused and sorrowful, not knowing what was going to happen, and unable to take on board everything their Teacher was speaking about.

They discussed among themselves some of the things he was saying, so when he saw that they wanted to ask him questions he explained.

"Now is your time of grief, but I will see you again and you will rejoice, and no-one will take away your joy. In that day you will no longer ask me anything. My Father will give you whatever you ask in my name. Until now you have not asked for anything in my name. Ask and you will receive and your joy will be complete."

Finally, Jesus spoke plainly of his imminent departure.

"The Father Himself loves you because you have loved me, and have believed that I came from God. I came from the Father and entered the world; now I am leaving the world and going back to the Father."

He had brought the disciples to a clearer understanding.

"Now you are speaking clearly and without figures of speech," they said. "Now we can see that you know all things and that you do not even need to have anyone ask you questions. This makes us believe that you came from God."

"You believe at last!" Jesus answered.

255

Yes, they believed now, but in the great testing that they were about to face, would their faith hold strong? Jesus knew that their faith was weak. They knew he came from God, but the events that were about to take place would utterly shock and confuse them. They would be rocked to the core, and they would scatter and leave their Teacher all alone.

"Yet I am not alone," said Jesus, "for my Father is with me."

He would be the one facing the greatest testing, but he would not doubt.

His teaching finished, Jesus knew that he needed the strength that would come from communication with his Father, so as he stood still he looked up towards heaven and prayed. He was well aware of the inevitability of what would happen.

"Father, the time has come. Glorify your Son, that your Son may glorify you. For you granted him authority over all people that he might give eternal life to all those you have given him. Now this is eternal life: that they may know you, the only true

God, and Jesus Christ whom you have sent. I have brought you glory on earth by completing the work you gave me to do. And now Father, glorify me in your presence with the glory I had with you before the world began."

It was a succinct summary of the gospel story. The Son came from the Father to bring eternal life, fulfilling what was promised, and now he would return to God where he would enjoy the same status as he had with Him before the world began.

He prayed for his disciples.

"Holy Father, protect them by the power of your name – the name you gave me – so that they may be one as we are one."

That was the beauty of all that he had been teaching them. They would be one with each other and one with God the Father and Jesus the Son.

"My prayer is not that you take them out of the world but that you protect them from the Evil one," Jesus continued.

Oh yes, the Evil one would still be around! He would be crushed because he would lose the power over death, but he would still have the power to tempt and hurt until the time came when he would be completely and finally defeated.

At such a time, Jesus still thought of others. Not only did he pray for his disciples, but he prayed for all the people in the future who would believe in him.

"May they be brought to complete unity to let the world know that you sent me and have loved them even as you have loved me."

The final words of his beautiful prayer was for the encouragement of his disciples.

"Father, I want those you have given me to be with me where I am, and to see my glory, the glory you have given me because you loved me before the creation of the world."

Chapter 44

———— ✳ ————

The Garden of Gethsemane was a quiet olive grove close to the Mount of Olives. Jesus had come to it often for its peace and solitude, but tonight it was a place of anguish of soul. He knew his time had come.

The eleven disciples accompanied him. Jesus invited Peter, James and John to join with him a short distance away, to provide the support of close friends as he agonized over his coming trial.

"My soul is overwhelmed with sorrow to the point of death," he said. "Stay here and keep watch with me."

The enormity of what he must endure weighed heavily on him. He would die a horrible death, but that was not even the worst. He must bear the sins of the whole world on his shoulders, all the heinous sins of sinful mankind, all the wickedness of hatred, murder, greed, all the iniquities known to man.

Going a little further into the shadows, he prayed with his face to the ground, being in agony.

"My Father, if it is possible, may this cup be taken from me. Yet not my will, but as you will."

The cup of sorrow he had undertaken to drink was a bitter cup, and he longed with all his being that he may not have to drink it. As it was, he was at the point of death with sorrow and anguish. He needed the support of his friends to pray for him and stand with him in his hour of need, but when he returned to them he found them sleeping. It deeply disappointed him.

To Peter he said, "Could you men not keep watch with me for one hour? Watch and pray so that you will not fall into temptation. The spirit is willing but the body is weak."

He went away again, about a stone's throw from them, close enough for them to hear and see.

"My Father, if it is not possible for this cup to be taken away unless I drink it, your will be done."

At this point an angel from heaven appeared and strengthened him. Still, his anguish was intense and he prayed even more earnestly.

Being in torment, his sweat was like great drops of blood falling to the ground. He was almost at the point of death through sheer sorrow and distress. This was the plan which he and his Father had made to save the world, and restore what was lost in the Garden of Eden, but it was such a costly plan. Here in the Garden of Gethsemane Jesus was faced with that cost.

For the third time he went away and prayed, saying the same words.

"Father, everything is possible for you. Take this cup from me. Yet not what I will, but what you will."

How could the Father cause him to suffer, and how could the Son be willing to go through with it?

Out of love. Such love! Supreme, divine love which none of us will ever be able to fathom.

The words of the prophet Isaiah were coming to pass.

"It was the Lord's will to crush him and cause him to suffer."

Why? Because "the Lord has laid on him the iniquity of us all."

When Jesus had finished praying, and had been sustained by the angel, he knew it was his Father's will that he would go through with the plan, so he returned to the still-sleeping disciples.

"The hour is near," he told them. "The Son of Man is betrayed into the hands of sinners. Rise, let us go! Here comes my betrayer!"

Chapter 45

———— ✳ ————

The night was dark. As Jesus now stood waiting with his disciples in the quiet garden they could see the lights of torches and lanterns coming towards them, and the quietness was broken by the hub-bub of voices.

Judas went up to him immediately, kissing him.

"Greetings Rabbi!" he said.

"Judas, are you betraying the Son of Man with a kiss?" Jesus asked sadly.

The son of perdition, as the disciples later described him, could make no reply.

"Friend, do what you came for," Jesus said.

Then he faced the crowd and asked, "Who is it you want?"

"Jesus of Nazareth," they replied.

"I am he," Jesus said simply.

In shock, or perhaps convicted by a power greater than themselves, they all fell backwards. They had come face to face with the Son of God and they were not able to withstand him.

Again Jesus asked, "Who is it you want?"

"Jesus of Nazareth," they said again.

"I told you that I am he," Jesus repeated. "If you are looking for me, then let these men go."

At that the crowd, made up of chief priests, elders, religious leaders, Pharisees and a detachment of soldiers from the Temple Guard, surged forward.

Jesus spoke to them. "Am I leading a rebellion, that you have come with swords and clubs? Every day I was with you in the Temple courts, and you did not lay a hand on me. But this is your hour – when darkness reigns.

The disciples, saddened, perplexed and fearful disappeared quickly into the dark night. Only Peter and John followed as Jesus was led away, Peter at a distance because he was afraid, yet propelled onward by a fascinated horror to see what would become of Jesus.

His captors took Jesus to the home of the high priest where many of the elders and teachers of the Law had assembled. It was late at night, but their best chance of convicting him was during the hours of darkness, before the general populace were up and about when they might have attempted to stop them.

Even now, it is incredible to think that the chief priests and religious leaders were actually looking for false evidence against Jesus, so that they could put him to death; false, because they knew they could find no true evidence which could condemn him.

Their tactics were flawed right from the start, and although many false witnesses came forward, their testimonies did not agree and the scheme all but failed.

Finally two witnesses did almost agree on something they had heard him say.

"This fellow said, 'I am able to destroy the temple of God and rebuild it in three days'," they declared.

The high priest seized on this flimsy piece of so-called evidence, and, standing up he said to Jesus, "Are you not going to answer? What is this testimony that these men are bringing against you?"

Jesus remained silent. Another of Isaiah's many prophecies came to fulfillment: "As a sheep before her shearers is silent, so he did not open his mouth."

Angry at his silence the high priest said sternly, "I charge you under oath by the living God: tell us if you are the Messiah, the Son of God."

"I am," said Jesus. "And you will see the Son of Man sitting at the right hand of the Mighty One and coming on the clouds of heaven."

The high priest tore his clothes. This was a long-standing traditional reaction which indicated that the word received was not good.

"Why do we need any more witnesses?" he demanded. "You have heard the blasphemy. What do you think?"

At once they all condemned him as worthy of death.

They had achieved their goal, they had a successful conviction. Now they would get rid of him for ever, and all would be well! Their place and their nation would be secure!

Oh, how foolish they were! He had confirmed that he was the Son of God. One day he would come on the clouds of heaven and they would see and know. Who would want to be in their shoes?

But now was their time. They had him trapped and this time he would not escape. Despised and condemned to death, he was insulted and mocked, beaten and tortured throughout the night hours of that dark day.

His disciple, John was watching but was helpless to aid him. As an eye-witness he was later able to record the details.

Peter too was there in the outer court. He had vehemently declared that he would not leave or deny Jesus, but Jesus knew better.

"Before the cock crows today, you will deny three times that you know me," Jesus had told him earlier that evening.

Poor weak, impetuous Peter! Three times, when asked by servants, he had sworn he had nothing to do with Jesus. When the cock crowed the second time, the Lord, in the midst of his ordeal, turned and looked at Peter, and Peter remembered. Going outside he wept bitterly.

Meanwhile the Son of God stood meekly among his tormentors until the dawn broke.

Chapter 46

———— ✳ ————

*A*lthough the religious leaders had condemned Jesus to death, they knew they
could not carry out the death sentence themselves.
Only the Romans could do that, so very early in
the morning they bound Jesus, and the whole
assembly took him to Pilate, the Roman Governor.

Hypocrites that they were, these religious
leaders would not enter the Palace, because they
wanted to remain ritually clean in order to par-
take of the Passover later that day, so Pilate con-
descended to come out to them.

"What charges are you bringing against this
man?" he asked.

"If he were not a criminal, we would not have handed him over to you," they replied indignantly.

A criminal? The sinless Son of God who had done only good, never any evil!

"Take him yourselves and judge him by your own law," Pilate retorted.

"But we have no right to execute anyone," they said, determined to push for the death penalty.

So Pilate had no choice but to go back inside the Palace and question Jesus.

"Are you the king of the Jews?" he asked abruptly.

"Is that your own idea, or did others talk to you about me?" Jesus asked.

"Am I a Jew?" asked Pilate sarcastically. "It was your people and your chief priests who handed you over to me. What is it you have done?"

"My kingdom is not of this world," Jesus explained. "If it were, my servants would fight to prevent my arrest. But now my kingdom is from another place."

"You are a king then?" asked Pilate.

"You are right in saying I am a king," Jesus acknowledged. "In fact, for this reason I was born, and for this reason I came into the world, to testify to the truth. Everyone on the side of truth listens to me."

"What is truth? asked Pilate cryptically, and without waiting for an answer he strode out again to the waiting Jews.

"I find no basis for a charge against him," he announced.

But they were not going to give up.

Determinedly they said, "He stirs up the people all over Judea by his teaching. He started in Galilee and has come all the way here."

When Pilate heard that Jesus was a Galilean, he sent him to King Herod since Galilee was his jurisdiction. It gave him the perfect opportunity to pass the decision regarding the fate of this young Rabbi to someone else.

So Jesus was taken to Herod who, as it happened, was greatly pleased to see him because he had heard of him and hoped to see him perform a miracle.

Vehemently the religious leaders continued to accuse him, but Jesus remained silent. If he had chosen to defend himself he would have demonstrated that their claims were false, and according to Judaic Law this would have had serious implications for them. The Law stated that "if the witness proves to be a liar, giving false testimony against his brother, then do to him as he intended to do to his brother." By saying nothing in his own defense Jesus took their sin upon himself. The accusers hated, but the accused loved enough to give his life for them.

Herod, disappointed and disgusted that he could draw no response from Jesus, decided to return him to Pilate. He handed him over to his soldiers who mocked and ridiculed him before escorting him back to the Roman Governor.

Pilate was deeply disturbed to see Jesus back again, because he knew in his heart that he was innocent, and had shrewdly concluded that the religious leaders wanted rid of him to serve their own ends. Consequently he did all he could to try and save him. Gathering together all the leaders he tried to reason with them.

"You brought this man to me as one who was inciting the people to rebellion," he told them. "I have examined him in your presence, and have found no basis for your charge against him. Neither has Herod, for he sent him back to us; as you can see he has done nothing to deserve death. Therefore I will punish him and then release him."

"Away with this man!" they shouted as one voice. "Release Barabbas to us."

It was customary for the Governor to release one prisoner at the time of the Passover Feast, one of the people's choosing, and Pilate desperately wanted to release Jesus, but the leaders persuaded the crowd, who by this time had gathered, to ask for Barabbas, who actually was a leader of a rebellion and a murderer.

Pilate tried again.

"Which one do you want me to release to you: Barabbas or Jesus who is called Messiah?"

"Barabbas," they shouted.

"What shall I do with Jesus who is called Messiah?" Pilate asked, each time trying to make the point that Jesus was their Messiah.

With one accord they yelled, "Crucify him!"

"Why?" asked Pilate incredulously. "What crime has he committed?"

He had committed no crime. As Isaiah had prophesied centuries earlier, "He had done no violence, nor was any deceit in his mouth."

Still the leaders shouted, "Crucify, crucify!" and there was such an uproar that Pilate could see he was getting nowhere. There was a tangible atmosphere of hatred and fury now among the crowd, whipped up by the vehemence of the chief priests, elders and Pharisees.

Oh, how they despised him! He was a Lawbreaker, he had dared to set himself against their authority, he was claiming to be the Son of God

– he, an uneducated carpenter from Nazareth. He must die! Nothing less would satisfy them.

Pilate took Jesus back inside and ordered him flogged. He reasoned that if he scourged him it would satisfy his accusers and prevent the death of an innocent man.

A Roman scourging was a ghastly affair. It scarcely bears thinking about, and in addition the Roman soldiers, hardened to dealing with the torture and death that was part of their lives, had no compunction about treating their prisoners harshly.

They had heard Jesus described as a king, so they gave him a crown – of thorns.

A purple robe was the raiment of kings, so they put one on him.

A king carried a sceptre, so they placed a staff in his hand.

"Hail, king of the Jews!" they mocked as they struck him again and again.

In their ignorance they demonstrated his king-ship, but only out of derision. The "sceptre had

come to whom it belonged" as Jacob had prophesied long years gone. Everything that was written
about him was coming to pass right before their
eyes and they did not know it.

Pilate brought him out to the crowd. He was
a pitiful sight, his back lacerated by the stripes,
thorns cutting deeply into his face, his eyes weary
with sleeplessness, pain and sorrow.

"Behold the man!" said Pilate, hoping against
hope that they would be satisfied that he had been
sufficiently punished. But no pity stirred in the
hearts of the religious leaders.

"Crucify, crucify!" they shouted again and again.

"You take him and crucify him," snapped Pilate
curtly. "As for me, I find no basis for a charge
against him."

"We have a law," insisted the leaders, "and
according to that law he must die, because he
claimed to be the Son of God."

Pilate's heart filled anew with fear on hearing
this, and he took Jesus back inside the palace to
question him more closely.

"Where do you come from?" he probed.

Jesus made no reply.

"Do you refuse to speak to me?" Pilate asked insistently. "Don't you realize I have power either to free you or to crucify you?"

To this Jesus did reply to let Pilate know that the power was not, as he thought, in his hands. The entire matter was in God's hands.

"You would have no power over me if it were not given to you from above. Therefore the one who handed me over to you is guilty of a greater sin."

This caused Pilate to become even more fearful, and he tried every way he could to set Jesus free, but the religious leaders were determined and cunning.

"If you let this man go, you are no friend of Caesar. Anyone who claims to be a king opposes Caesar," they said craftily.

This touched a nerve in Pilate. He was Roman and he owed allegiance to his own Emperor. Could he fail to condemn someone who was said to be a king, even though Jesus had led no rebellion in opposition to Caesar? But on the other hand, he feared the guilt of sending this prisoner to his death if he really was who he claimed to be.

One solution presented itself to him. He would wash his hands of it, literally, and declare himself free of blame, so he called for a basin of water to be brought to him, and he washed his hands in front of the crowd.

"I am innocent of this man's blood," he said firmly. "It is your responsibility."

Without a second thought the chief priests and leaders took the charge upon themselves.

"Let his blood be upon us and on our children," they shouted.

Pilate took his place on the judgement seat and tried one more time.

"Here is your king," he said.

"Take him away! Take him away! Crucify him!" they yelled, vehement as ever.

"Shall I crucify your king?" asked Pilate, in one last attempt to change their minds and save Jesus from death.

But they had an answer ready!

"We have no king but Caesar," they shouted.

They hated the Roman occupation. They did not want Caesar as king, but neither did they want this man Jesus as their king. Their opposition to him was so strong that they were prepared to compromise their own patriotism, and declare allegiance to an occupying Emperor rather than allow Jesus to live.

The irony of it! And the injustice of it!

Finally Pilate could see it was useless, and he chose to come down on the side of Rome. Reluctantly he pronounced the death penalty, and handed Jesus over to be crucified. The religious leaders had had their way.

Chapter 47

The journey through the narrow shadowed streets

Led at last to dread Golgotha,

Where craggy rock and stark white stone

Fashioned the rugged outline of a skull.

There he was crucified.

There they nailed his hands and feet

And pierced his side.

There, Jesus died.

There were many at the foot of the cross who witnessed the grim scene: the jubilant religious leaders who had got what they wanted, the curious onlookers–many shocked, some derisive, the indifferent soldiers who gambled for his clothing.

Then there were the women who knew him and loved him, those who had been touched by his healing power and his compassion. Mary, his mother, whose heart was pierced as by a sword, stood along with John, alone of all his disciples who came.

The sign above his cross, placed there on Pilate's orders, read, "Jesus of Nazareth, the king of the Jews." The chief priests complained at its wording but Pilate refused to change it.

"What I have written I have written," he said.

Along with Jesus two robbers were also cruci- fied, one on either side of him. The Scriptures were fulfilled where they said, "He was numbered with the transgressors."

Isaiah's poignant passages were completely accurate.

"He was pierced for our transgressions; He was bruised for our iniquities. The punishment that brought us peace was upon him, and by his wounds we are healed."

Jesus himself said very little as others were mocking and sneering at him. Only gracious words came from his lips.

"Father, forgive them for they do not know what they are doing."

He could forgive while they could only deride. He loved his people, all of them.

One of the robbers, in repentance said, "Jesus, remember me when you come into your kingdom."

"Today you will be with me in paradise," Jesus told him.

As he looked down at his heart-broken mother standing with his only faithful disciple, Jesus understood their sorrow and spoke to comfort them.

"Dear woman, here is your son," he said to Mary, and to John, "Here is your mother."

They now had each other for comfort.

As the hours passed the pain, the sorrow and the burden of the world's sins which he carried became too great to bear.

"My God, my God, why have You forsaken me?" he cried in anguish, the words coming from David's prophetic Psalm.

It was the weight of the world's sins which separated him for a time from his Father. He had taken our sin upon himself, acting as our substitute. As Isaiah said, "The Lord has laid on him the iniquity of us all", and a holy God could not look upon such awful sin.

It was this that had caused him such agony in the Garden of Gethsemane, and it was this that cost both his Father and himself so dearly. To us it is a mystery, and we will never be able to fathom either the holiness of God or the love of God for His creation. We can only say that He hates sin but loves the sinner, and that is why Jesus was willing to go to the cross.

Although it was still afternoon, darkness descended over the whole land. It was the darkest day the world had ever known. The Lamb of God was dying and the blackness was fitting.

With his life ebbing away, David's prophetic words were so appropriate.

"I am poured out like water, and all my bones are out of joint.

My heart has turned to wax; it has melted away within me.

My strength has dried up like a potsherd,

And my tongue sticks to the roof of my mouth."

"I am thirsty," he managed to gasp.

They gave him wine vinegar. It enabled him to utter the vital triumphant words, "It is finished."

His work was done. He had "poured out his life unto death", he had paid the price, he had accomplished our atonement.

"Father, into Your hands I commit my spirit."

He was gone, and at that moment the curtain into the Holy of Holies in the Temple was torn in two from top to bottom. There would be no more need of a priest to enter there on behalf of anyone. Jesus had put an end to sacrificial offerings by the sacrifice of himself, and had atoned for wickedness. The prophecies had been fulfilled.

Darkness had covered the land for the last three hours, but now there was an earthquake, the earth shaking and the rocks splitting, even the tombs opening, and believing people who had died were raised to life. It was a dramatic action by Almighty God who wanted the world to know that something stupendous had taken place.

The Roman centurion in charge was deeply stirred. It drew a striking admission from him.

"Truly, this man was the Son of God."

The religious leaders, always keen to uphold the Law, wanted the bodies taken down from the crosses before the Sabbath, so they asked Pilate to have the legs broken so that they would die quickly and their bodies could be taken down.

The soldiers broke the legs of the two robbers, but when they saw that Jesus was already dead they pierced his side instead with a spear which caused a sudden flow of blood and water.

The Scriptures were fulfilled!

"Not one of his bones will be broken." It was a Passover restriction. None of the bones of the sacrificial Passover lamb were to be broken.

There is so much strong significance in everything surrounding the death of the Saviour. He was truly "the Lamb of God who takes away the sin of the world."

Another Scripture says, "They will look on the one they have pierced."

Everything that was written about him came to pass.

Chapter 48

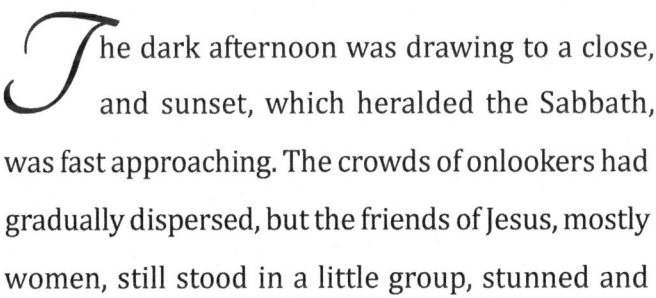

The dark afternoon was drawing to a close, and sunset, which heralded the Sabbath, was fast approaching. The crowds of onlookers had gradually dispersed, but the friends of Jesus, mostly women, still stood in a little group, stunned and scarcely able to take in the events of the past few hours. They wondered what would happen next.

Not all the members of the Sanhedrin had agreed to the death penalty for Jesus. A man called Joseph from the Judean town of Arimathea was a good and upright man, a secret follower of Jesus, and he had not consented to their decision. Now he knew it was time to take a stand, so boldly he went to Pilate and asked for the body of Jesus.

Nicodemus, who by now was also a believer, brought myrrh and other spices, so the two men carefully wrapped the body in linen cloths with the spices to prepare him for burial.

Joseph was a wealthy man and he had already prepared a burial place for himself, a tomb cut into the rock in a quiet garden. Here they decided to place Jesus' body since it was close by, and it was now near the start of the Sabbath.

It fulfilled Isaiah's prophecy that Jesus would be "assigned a grave with the rich in his death." They rolled a large stone against the tomb, leaving it secure before they left.

The women were watching carefully. They saw where the body of Jesus was laid, and they determined that after the Sabbath they would come back and add more spices, perhaps also wanting to return and look once more upon their beloved friend and Lord.

When they had taken note of the place they went home.

Chapter 49

———— ✳ ————

*I*t was not yet sunrise, but the Son had risen! Dramatically, powerfully, triumphantly the Son of God arose from the grave!

An angel, whose appearance was like lightening, had descended from heaven, and in the earthquake which followed, the great heavy stone which sealed the tomb was dislodged, leaving the tomb open. The angel then sat upon the stone.

The terrified guards, placed there to watch the tomb, shook violently, rooted to the spot with fear. When they finally recovered themselves sufficiently, some of them ran into the city to report what had happened, and were paid to say that the disciples had come at night time while they were sleeping and had stolen the body.

It was still dark when Mary Magdalene and the other women made their way to the garden tomb. While they walked they discussed the heavy stone which sealed the entrance. Who would move it for them?

As they entered the quiet garden dawn was breaking, and they noticed immediately that the stone had already been moved. Strange! When they reached the tomb they looked inside. It was empty! Jesus was not there!

As the women looked at each other wonderingly they became aware of two angels standing beside them. Their presence and the brilliance of their appearance was overwhelming, filling the women with a sense of shock and fear.

"Do not be afraid," said the angel, "For I know that you are looking for Jesus, who was crucified. He is not here; he has risen just as he said. Come and see the place where they laid him."

The women looked. The strips of linen which had bound his body were lying on the stone slab, and the cloth that had been around his head was folded and lying separately. Mystified, they looked up at the angel again, who continued.

"Go and tell his disciples: He has risen from the dead and is going ahead of you into Galilee. There you will see him. Now, I have told you."

So the women hurried away, trembling yet filled with joy at this momentous news. They had seen with their own eyes that the tomb was empty, and had heard what the angel had said.

"He is not here: he has risen!"

It was glorious news! They must tell the disciples at once.

The disciples, sorrowful and dispirited, were not impressed with the news which the women brought. They simply did not believe them.

Nevertheless, Peter and John decided to check it out. They ran to the tomb, and sure enough found it empty. John initially looked in but did not go in. Peter did go in and noted the grave clothes lying there, but he went away again, wondering to himself.

John did not leave with Peter, but moved by a strong impulse he entered the tomb. As he gazed at the linen grave cloths lying there with the burial cloth which had been around Jesus' head folded and lying by itself, he knew within himself that it was true. Jesus had arisen!

Meanwhile Mary Magdalene stood outside the tomb weeping. Her love for the Lord was deep. He had done so much for her.

The angels asked her, "Woman why are you crying?"

"They have taken my Lord away, and I don't know where they have put him," she said.

As she turned away, blinded by her tears, another voice spoke.

"Woman, why are you crying? Who is it you are looking for?"

Thinking he was the gardener she begged him to tell her where he had put the body.

"Mary," said Jesus softly.

She knew instantly it was Jesus by the way he spoke her name.

"Rabboni!" she exclaimed joyously, falling at his feet.

"Do not hold on to me," said Jesus gently, "for I have not yet returned to the Father. Go instead to my brothers and tell them, 'I am returning to my Father and your Father, to my God and your God."

Mary left at once with the news.

"I have seen the Lord!" she announced jubilantly.

She was the first to see him after his resurrection, but soon they would all see him and know that he was alive. Death could not hold him, for God did not abandon him to the grave. He had raised him from the dead!

Chapter 50

*I*t had all begun in a garden. Everything had changed there, but God had a plan and He made a promise. The Son of the Promise had come, had lived, died and had risen to life again. Satan had been crushed, death had been defeated. The beautiful garden of the tomb was the scene of the Resurrection. It had come full circle.

Throughout that wonderful day the word spread quickly among Jesus' friends and his eleven disciples that the tomb was empty and that he was alive. So far only Mary Magdalene and some of the other women had been privileged to see him. They had told of seeing the shining angels who gave them the news, and how the Lord himself had greeted them in the garden.

As evening approached two friends who were followers of Jesus, left Jerusalem to return to their village of Emmaus. As they walked they talked with such intense concentration of all the events which had taken place over the last few days that they were scarcely aware that someone had joined them.

"What are you discussing together as you walk along?" he asked.

With eyes downcast they still did not know who was walking with them, so they explained that a prophet called Jesus of Nazareth had been crucified and that it was now the third day since this had happened.

"Some of our women amazed us," they concluded. "They went to the tomb early this morning but did not find his body. They came and told us they had seen a vision of angels, who said he was alive. Then some of our companions went to the tomb and found it just as the women had said, but him they did not see."

"How foolish you are, and how slow of heart to believe all that the prophets have spoken!" Jesus said to them.

Then, beginning with Moses and all the Prophets he explained how everything they had written relating to the Messiah had come to pass.

When they arrived at their home, Jesus made as if he would go on, but as it was late they wanted to offer him hospitality so they urged him to stay with them.

As they sat down to supper, Jesus took bread in his hands and gave thanks, broke it and gave it to them. In this familiar little action they recognized him, and before they knew it he disappeared out of their sight.

They were so excited that they immediately set out for Jerusalem, late as it was, to tell his disciples that Jesus was alive.

The disciples were gathered together behind locked doors, still fearful that they might be arrested, especially now that the news of the empty tomb had reached the authorities. They knew they could be blamed for taking his body, but that would have been impossible to them, fearful as they were and with guards posted beside the tomb.

Suddenly, in spite of locked doors, Jesus stood among them.

"Peace be with you," he said.

At first they were startled at the suddenness of his appearance, thinking they had seen a ghost.

"Why are you troubled, and why do doubts arise in your minds?" Jesus asked. "Look at my hands and feet. It is I myself! Touch me and see; a ghost does not have flesh and bones, as you see I have."

They were filled with joy and amazement as they gazed at him. They gave him some food and he ate it in front of them. Their joy knew no bounds.

"This is what I told you while I was still with you," he said. "Everything must be fulfilled that is written about me in the Law of Moses, the Prophets and the Psalms."

He began to open up the Scriptures to them, and as he spoke their minds became receptive so that they understood what he was saying.

"This is what is written," he said. "The Messiah will suffer and rise from the dead on the third day, and repentance and forgiveness of sins will be preached in his name to all nations, beginning at Jerusalem. You are witnesses of these things. I am going to send you what my Father has promised; but stay in the city until you have been clothed with power from on high."

He was speaking of the Holy Spirit which he promised he would send. The Spirit would give them the power they needed to go out and spread the gospel. They were to wait in Jerusalem until the Holy Spirit came into the world and made His dwelling within them

He had a special commission for his disciples which he gave them when he met with them in Galilee. On the mountain where Jesus had arranged to meet with them he talked to them about what he wanted them to do.

"All authority in heaven and on earth has been given to me," he told them. "Therefore go and make disciples of all nations, baptizing them in the name of the Father and of the Son and of the Holy Spirit, and teaching them to obey everything I have commanded you. And surely I am with you always, to the very end of the age."

In the forty days Jesus remained on earth after his resurrection, he spent time not only with his disciples, but he met with many others as well. Hundreds of Jewish people, including some of the religious leaders, had believed in him, and rejoiced to see him arisen from the dead.

The gospel writers have written all the important facts as eye witnesses, but it would be lovely to use one's imagination and visualize how wonderful it would have been for Martha, Mary and Lazarus, for example, to see him, or Joseph and Nicodemus who had kindly and bravely taken charge of his body, or Mary his mother who would see him again alive and well. How happy they must have been!

But we must stick to facts, and they are all there. He was born, lived, died and was raised from the dead as the prophets foretold, and as the eye-witnesses recorded. He arose! The empty tomb was the proof. There was no body that the authorities could produce. He was alive! He moved about at will among his own followers. Unbelievers did not see him. They had had their chance, but did not take it, and so they did not see the risen Lord.

When the time came to leave the earth Jesus led his eleven disciples out of the city.

"You will receive power when the Holy Spirit comes on you; and you will be my witnesses in Jerusalem, and in all Judea and Samaria, and to the ends of the earth."

These were his last words to them on earth. Immediately after this he was taken up from them in the clouds into his abode in heaven with his Father.

As they watched him go, two angels appeared beside them.

"Men of Galilee," they said. "Why do you stand here looking into the sky? This same Jesus, who has been taken up into heaven, will come back in the same way as you have seen him go into heaven."

They remembered his words at the last supper he had with them.

"I will come back and take you to be with me that you also may be where I am."

The Son of the Promise had promised, and he would fulfill that promise!

Come, Lord Jesus!

Bible References for Quotations used

————— ※ —————

1 Mal. 4: 2 Hag. 2: 7 Amos 9: 11

Hab. 2: 14

Chapter 16   Ez. 1: 28 Ez. 18: 30-32 Ez. 37: 3-4

Ez. 37: 22-25, 26

Chapter 17   Zech. 2: 10 Zech. 6: 12 Zech. 9: 9, 10

Zech. 12: 10-12 Zech. 13: 1, 6, 7

Zech. 14: 4, 5, 9

Chapter 18   2 Chron. 32: 7-8 Micah 5: 2

Chapter 19   Dan. 9: 22, 24-26 Is. 45: 13

Dan. 9: 26 Dan. 12: 4

Chapter 20   Gal. 4: 4

Chapter 21   Luke 1: 30-38, 42-45, 46-49, 54-55,

68, 76-77 Matt. 1: 20-21 Micah 5: 2

Chapter 22   Luke 2: 10-12, 14, 15

Chapter 23   Luke 2:29, 34

Chapter 24   Matt. 2: 2 Micah 5:2 Luke 2: 8

Is. 60: 3 Matt. 2: 23

Chapter 25   Matt. 3: 11 Luke 1: 76 John 1: 20-23

Matt. 3: 14-15 Mark 1: 11

John 1: 26, 32-34

Chapter 26   John 1: 29, 30-31, 35, 41, 43, 45-49

Chapter 27   Is. 61: 1-2 Like 4: 18 Luke 4: 21

Mark 6: 2

Chapter 28   Matt. 5: 3, 4, 13, 14, 17, 43-44, 48

Matt. 6: 3, 8, 9-13, 19-20, 25-27

Gen. 8:22 Matt. 6: 28-30, 33

Matt. 7: 1-3, 7-8, 12, 13

Chapter 29   John 3: 2, 3, 5, 9, 13, 14

Num. 21: 6-9 John 3: 16, 17

Chapter 30   John 8: 4-5, 7, 10-11 Mark 2: 17

Luke 5: 20-26

Chapter 31   Matt. 22: 36-39 Matt. 6: 5

John 5: 24, 33, 37, 39-40, 46

Deut. 18: 18 John 5: 47 John 5: 40

Chapter 32   Luke 7: 13-16 Luke 19: 5, 7-10

John 6: 47

Chapter 33   John 4: 9-26, 29, 42

Chapter 34   Luke 15: 10 Luke 19: 10 John 14: 6

Luke 17: 20-21 Matt. 21: 28-32

Chapter 35   Matt. 21: 33-42 Matt. 22: 2-3, 12

Matt. 13: 24-26, 43 Matt 13: 31, 49

Chapter 36   John 1: 1-3 John 4: 49-50

John 5: 6-8 John 6: 14 John 8: 12

John 6: 20 Matt. 14: 27, 33

Chapter 37   John 9: 7, 9, 16, 17, 19, 21, 24-38

Chapter 38   John 10: 11, 16, 17-18 Is. 53: 6

John 10: 9-10, 14

Chapter 39   Luke 10: 40-42 John 11: 3-4, 8, 11,

15, 21-44, 47

Chapter 40   John 12: 7 Matt. 20: 18-19

Matt. 21: 2-5, 9-11, 15-16, 23-27

John 12: 19

Chapter 41   Mark 14: 12-15 John 13: 6-9, 13-14

Luke 22: 15-16, 17-20

John 13: 21 Matt. 26: 22

John 13: 25-27, 31, 33-34

Chapter 42   John 14: 1-6, 8-14, 16-20, 23, 25,

27, 30-31

Chapter 43   John 14: 31 John 15: 1-4, 9-13

John 16: 22-24, 27-28, 29-32

John 17: 1-5 John 17: 11, 15, 23, 24

Chapter 44   Matt. 26: 38-42 Mark 14: 36

Is. 53: 10, 6 Matt. 26: 45-46

Chapter 45   Matt. 26: 49 Luke 22: 48

Matt. 26: 50 John 18: 4-8

Luke 22: 52-53 Matt. 26: 61-63

Mark 14: 62-64 Luke 22: 34

Chapter 46   John 18: 29-31, 33-38

Luke 23: 5, 14-18 Matt. 27: 22-23,

29 John 19: 5-7 John 19: 9-11

Matt. 27: 24-25 John 19: 14-15

Chapter 47   John 19: 19-22 Is. 53: 12 Is. 53: 5

Luke 23: 34, 42-43 John 19: 26-27

Matt. 27: 46 Is. 53: 6 Ps. 22: 14-15

John 19: 28, 30 Luke 23: 46

Mark 15: 39 John 19: 36

(Ex. 12: 46) John 1: 29 Zech 12: 10

Chapter 48   Is. 53: 9

Chapter 49   Matt. 28: 5-7 Matt. 28: 6

John 20: 13-16, 18

Chapter 50   Luke 24: 17-24, 25

John 20: 19 Luke 24: 36-39, 44,

46-49 Matt. 28:18

Acts 1: 8, 11 John 14: 3

Lightning Source UK Ltd.
Milton Keynes UK
UKOW06f1102161016

285383UK00001B/15/P